Guildhall: City of London

Guildhall: City of London

History. Guide. Companion.

Graham Greenglass and Stephen Dinsdale

Illustrations by Mark Carter

PEN & SWORD
HISTORY

First published in Great Britain in 2018 and reprinted in this format in
2022 by
PEN AND SWORD HISTORY
an imprint of
Pen and Sword Books Ltd
47 Church Street
Barnsley
South Yorkshire S70 2AS

ISBN 978 1 52671 541 8

Printed and bound in the UK by CPI Group (UK) Ltd, Croydon, CRO 4YY

Typeset in Times New Roman 10/12.5 by
Aura Technology and Software Services, India

Pen & Sword Books Ltd incorporates the imprints of Pen & Sword
Archaeology, Atlas, Aviation, Battleground, Discovery,
Family History, History, Maritime, Military, Naval, Politics, Railways,
Select, Social History, Transport, True Crime, Claymore Press, Frontline
Books, Leo Cooper, Praetorian Press, Remember When, Seaforth
Publishing and Wharncliffe.

For a complete list of Pen and Sword titles please contact
Pen and Sword Books Limited
47 Church Street, Barnsley, South Yorkshire, S70 2AS, England
E-mail: enquiries@pen-and-sword.co.uk
Website: www.pen-and-sword.co.uk

Contents

Acknowledgements

For help, permissions and small acts of kindness, we would like to thank: Mick Bagnall, Susie Barson, Howard Benge, Tanya Dean, Andrew Ford, Doreen Golding, Elain Harwood, Leanne O'Boyle, Benjamin O'Connor, Peter Ross, Adrian Scarborough, Simon Stephenson, Dr Jackie Stirling, Peter Twist, Jerome Vincent, Lindsey Wishart and Deborah Murrell.

We have endeavoured to get permissions where required. If we have made any omissions it is unintentional and we would request contact is made so this can be rectified.

Foreword
by the Lord Mayor of the City of London

Just like the city in which it sits, the Guildhall has a complex and fascinating history. From the remains of the Roman amphitheatre which lies beneath it to the astounding architecture of the Great Hall, it is a symbol of London's governance, history and culture.

Dating back to 1411, the Great Hall has witnessed its fair share of drama – acting as both the setting for pomp and circumstance of state and mayoral occasions and a place in which peers, an archbishop and a queen were all tried for treason during the Reformation.

Today, the Guildhall's functions are more modern. It is both the home of the administration of the City of London Corporation, and used as a venue for significant City conferences on matters concerning the financial and professional services industry. Its mix of history and modernity, tradition and entrepreneurship, is symbolic of the wider spirit of the City of London.

Exploring in greater detail the history, art and architecture of the Guildhall, this book will reveal some of the City's forgotten stories, the people behind them and how events at the Guildhall have influenced the formation of Britain's capital today.

I trust you contemplate and celebrate *Guildhall: City of London.*

Alderman Charles Bowman, The Rt Hon the Lord Mayor of the City of London, 2017-2018.

Lord Mayor's Show 2017. Permission of the Office of the Lord Mayor.

Introduction

The hidden gem in the heart of the City of London is Guildhall. An often used, much abused phrase that, hidden gem. It requires explanation.

Guildhall is the town hall of the City of London. It is a large complex of buildings hidden between Gresham Street, Basinghall Street and Aldermansbury. So well hidden that it's barely visible from any of the City streets we've just mentioned.

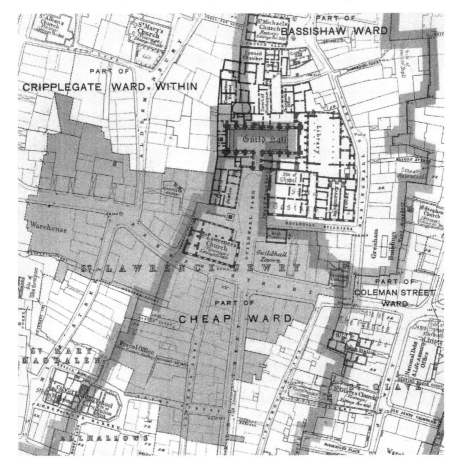

Cheap Ward 1855.

The epicentre of this inter-connected assemblage of buildings is the Great Hall: Perpendicular Gothic, 600 years old and despite being burned during the Great Fire of 1666 and bombed during the Blitz in 1940, its glory years have never actually ended.

It has served variously as the ceremonial centre of the City and a court room, military recruitment centre and banqueting hall, public space and mercantile powerhouse. It has hosted kings and queens, presidents and prime ministers, political rallies and financial fraternities.

Coronation Banquet, 1953.

INTRODUCTION

The Great Hall's symbolic custodian is the Lord Mayor of the City of London. Each new monarch will be invited to a coronation banquet and every visiting head of state entertained at a state banquet, all hosted by the Lord Mayor. Every November each new Lord Mayor will themselves be guest of honour at their own banquet.

To the east of Guildhall Yard, abutting the Great Hall, is the only public art gallery in the City, with its world-leading collection of British nineteenth century art. For those in the know and who venture beneath, within the gallery basement are the remains of Londinium's Roman amphitheatre.

Back at street level, hugging the west side of the Great Hall, is Guildhall's own West Wing: offices to the City of London Corporation and poster boy to a post-war architectural renaissance that swept London. The architect of Guildhall Art Gallery and West Wing, Richard Gilbert Scott, is last in a long line of London architects whose work has contributed to this site since the early fifteenth century. They include Christopher Wren, George Dance the Younger, Horace Jones and Gilbert Scott's own father Sir Giles Gilbert Scott.

Guildhall has its own library. The reference-only Guildhall Library is home to the world's largest collection of books dedicated to one city, that city of course being London. The Library's West Wing neighbour since 2016 has been the City of London Police Museum. From Charleys and Peelers to anarchist and IRA terror, a slice of City life is well illustrated in this new space dedicated to criminal history.

The City's past and future is represented too. The Heritage Gallery in the Art Gallery rotates documents and objects that have been pivotal in City history; and in the City Centre a remarkable model of the Square Mile's urban landscape illustrates in 3D the City streets and buildings of both today and the future. Public sculpture abounds in Guildhall Yard and to the north of the complex next to the administrative North Wing.

Finally, the people. What would these buildings be were it not for the people that have shaped their history and the spirit that lives within them. So not just a hidden gem, but host to very real stories of power, pageantry, punishment and progress.

This book aims to be all things Guildhall. It's a history, a guide and a companion. We hope it will be useful for the student of City life, Guildhall explorer, tourist or curious Londoner.

Chapter 1

Early History

Many towns in the United Kingdom have guildhalls. They are usually just called 'The Guildhall'. London's Guildhall is often referred to simply as 'Guildhall' but nobody seems to know why. It is just one of the mysteries surrounding this extraordinary building.

London was founded by the Romans. Before they arrived there was no significant settlement where London is now. Archaeologists have found some evidence of scattered pre-Roman human habitation but, as far as we know up to this point, nothing significant to speak of. Julius Caesar did not mention anything in his writings.

The founding of London was not in 55 BC when Caesar first came and famously said 'I came, I saw, I conquered,' but around a hundred years later in AD 43 when Emperor Claudius decided to mount a full invasion, led by general Aulus Plautius.

The Romans settled where London is now for several reasons. It was the lowest bridgeable spot on the River Thames, the site provided a good natural harbour for their ships and the river was tidal up to the London area. It would be useful as a landing place for troops to further the invasion of Britain and also for trade between the province of Britannia and Rome. The river provided a good defence should there be an attack from the south. There were also some hills to the north which could be settled and provide useful defensive positions against any attack that might come from that direction.

The Roman city of Londinium was founded roughly where the modern City of London – the Square Mile – is today. Remains of the earliest settlement, from around AD 47, were found under the building No 1 Poultry. There was a break in development in AD 60 when Boudicca, the Queen of the Iceni tribe in East Anglia, rebelled against the Romans after they betrayed her. She destroyed Camulodunum (Colchester), Verulamium (St Albans) and burned down Londinium. She and her armies were later defeated, and archaeologists call this early layer the 'Boudiccan destruction horizon'. After her attack the city was rebuilt. There is an unproved myth that she may be buried under King's Cross Station.

There is also a mythical story of London's first origins, in which it was founded by Brutus of Troy. The myth starts with the Roman emperor Diocletian, who had thirty-three daughters. The eldest was called Alba. Diocletian found husbands for his daughters but, goaded on by Alba, the daughters killed the husbands. To punish them Diocletian put them on a boat with six month's supply of food and sent them out to sea. They arrived at an island, Britain, populated by giants. They named it Albion after older sister Alba, and the sisters and the giants between them produced another race of giants.

The myth continues that Brutus of Troy landed on Albion. He was said to be a descendent of Aeneas, a hero of the Trojan Wars. After the fall of Troy, when the ancient Greeks sacked the city using their wooden horse, Aeneas journeyed to Italy. Brutus was born there, but killed his parents and was exiled. After some wanderings with his followers he came to Albion, which is now named Britain after him.

Here Brutus founded a city on the site of London named New Troy, his palace where Guildhall is now. He fought with the giants of Albion for control of Britain. There are different versions of these battles. One story is that two of the giants, Gog and Magog were defeated, taken prisoner and brought to New Troy where they acted as guardians of the palace. The myth persisted and they are represented by the statues of Gog and Magog in Guildhall's Great Hall. Another version of the

Left and opposite:
Gog and Magog,
carved by Richard
Saunders in 1709. Each
stood thirteen feet tall.
Destroyed in the Blitz,
29 December 1940.

Another legendary founder of London was King Lud. Ludgate is named after him.

legend is that the Magog figure in the Great Hall is that of Corineus, a warrior who joined Brutus of Troy in his wanderings and helped him defeat the giants. None of the Brutus of Troy story is true. It is all legend, but it was generally thought to be the truth until the sixteenth century and by some even after that.

To return to the true story of London, it was rebuilt after Boudicca's attack and had a good complement of Roman amenities – such as a forum, baths, Governor's house and basilica. Archaeologists have found evidence of all of these. However, one thing seemed to be missing. A Roman city the size of Londinium should have had an amphitheatre, and there was not any archaeological evidence of one. During the Second World War the Guildhall Art Gallery was bombed and after the war it was decided to build a new one. After some delay, work began and the foundations were sunk – and in 1988 they found the remains of the Roman amphitheatre. The amphitheatre and art gallery will be discussed in more detail in Chapter 10 and Chapter 12.

Towards the end of Roman occupation Londinium was under constant pressure from Anglo-Saxon raiding parties. The Romans finally left Britain, due to attacks on Rome, in AD 410. The Saxons did not occupy the Londinium buildings left by the Romans but created their own settlements in the area, mostly to the west, and as the centuries passed the myth grew that many of the old buildings that were left had been put there by giants.

The amphitheatre site was clearly seen as important though. It is thought the Saxons held their citizen's meetings or folkmoots there. The site was within the City walls, which had been re-fortified by King Alfred at the end of the ninth century, and perhaps on empty but still firm ground. This may have led to Guildhall eventually being built in the same area, as London within-the-walls fully re-established itself from the late Saxon period.

The word Guildhall suggests a connection with the guilds. These were, broadly speaking, trade organisations that were founded in the Middle Ages and are still flourishing today. The name 'Guild' may come from 'gield', an Old English word for 'pay tribute' and the original Guildhall might have been where taxes were collected. The word also comes from money – geld, gilt, gold.

If there was a direct connection to the guilds, there is a suggestion it might have been to the obscure Knighten Guild, which is mentioned by John Stow, the sixteenth century historian. The Knighten Guild was originally given special privileges by King Edward the Confessor in the eleventh century but was dissolved in the twelfth century and possibly absorbed by other guilds. Again, this is only a theory.

The original Guildhall was probably a small hall where the current west crypt is. Its other role was to host the ancient Court of Husting first mentioned in 1032 – though it was probably much older than that. This is where the Aldermen met, high-ranking officials whose name evolved from the Old English 'ealdorman' (the elder man), and was the supreme court dealing with administration and judicial matters. No records remain of the court, although we know it was held weekly by the mid-twelfth century. When the present Guildhall was finished in the fifteenth century they included the arms of Edward the Confessor (1042-1066), so they must have thought a building was there during his reign.

There was some sort of guildhall from around 1125, and by the reign of King John in the early thirteenth century there was a building that was the centre of administration. Very little is known about it. An 1128 summary of properties belonging to St Paul's Cathedral also mentions a guildhall.

A second Guildhall was built probably around 1270-90 and it is thought it had three rooms. There are references to meetings in the Chamber of Guildhall and this is also where the city's records and money were kept. Alterations were carried out in the 1320s and 1330s. It's thought that today's undercroft level was the ground floor, with the east end raised for a hustings (assembly) court – probably the present West Crypt. There may also have been an Upper Chamber and an Inner Chamber. The Common Council met in the Upper Chamber and the Mayor with the Court of Aldermen met in the Inner Chamber.

A chapel dedicated to God, St Mary, St Mary Magdalene and All Saints was built next to the Guildhall, to the south east, at the end of the thirteenth century.

The main entrance was on Guildhall Yard. It was also associated with the Society of Puy, a brotherhood of the educated and wealthy who were dedicated to make London known for all good things. In the mid-fourteenth century a college of five priests, with a garden, was built to the south of the chapel.

At the beginning of the fifteenth century the early Guildhall was more or less where the present one is. To the south was Guildhall Yard, with a gatehouse on its south side, giving onto Catte Street, later Cateaton Street, now Gresham Street. To the west of the gatehouse was the church of St Lawrence Jewry. To the east of the gatehouse was Blackwell estate and hall. Blackwell Hall was a large hall in which a cloth market took place, established in the late fourteenth century. To the north of Blackwell Hall on the east side of the Yard was the college of priests and next to that was the chapel.

One significant early event that took place in the old Guildhall was the celebration of the birth of the future King Edward III in 1312. The City of London held a festival for a week and in the last day of rejoicing the Mayor and Aldermen, all in their ceremonial robes, along with the Guilds of Vintners, Drapers and Mercers in their livery costumes, rode to Westminster to pay their respects. They then returned to Guildhall which was richly decorated and hung with tapestries. They had a banquet there and after dinner 'went in carols' through the City, for the rest of the day and long into the night.

King Edward III later went to war in France in what became known as The Hundred Years War. With the aid of City money his English armies defeated the French at the battles of Crécy and Poitiers. Before Crécy (1346) the City was worried

Guildhall Porch, Chapel and Blackwell Hall as it appeared in the 1820s.

about the possibility of a French invasion and protected Guildhall with 'guns wrought of latten mounted on teleres and charged with powder and pellets of lead'.

In 1363 under former Lord Mayor Henry Picard, the Vintners held a banquet for Edward III to celebrate his victories in France. Later the City played a part in the deposition of Edward's grandson, King Richard II. The accusations of his misgovernment were read out in Guildhall.

In the fifteenth century King Henry V continued the English claim to the throne of France. There was a meeting in Guildhall between the Mayor, the Dukes of Bedford, Gloucester and York, the Archbishop of Canterbury, the Bishop of Winchester and others to decide how the military campaign should be funded. This led to a question of precedence – who among all these dignitaries should chair the meeting? It was decided that the Mayor should, as the King's representative in the City. The precedent was set and has been kept to ever since.

The Great Hall of Guildhall as we now see it, probably the third on the site, was started by John Croxtone in 1411 and mostly completed by 1430 in the Perpendicular Gothic style of architecture. Croxtone was not an architect – the profession did not exist then – but a mason.

It is the oldest non-ecclesiastical building in the City of London and is a Grade One Listed Building – a building of exceptional interest. It was the second largest Great Hall covered by a single-span roof in medieval England. Only Westminster Hall at the Palace of Westminster (part of the Houses of Parliament) is larger. A contemporary source, Robert Fabyan, described the

John Croxtone.

6

previous Guildhall as 'an Olde and Lytell Cotage' but the new one he called a 'fayre and goodly house'.

The western crypt – the crypt from the earlier building – had been retained and a new eastern crypt was built. The western crypt was probably used for City business while the new Guildhall was being built. The windows were enlarged to enable its expanded use.

Croxtone's porch for the new building, on the south side, took the form of a large, elaborate church porch. The roof of the Great Hall was probably made of wood. There were two large windows, one at the west end and one at the east end. Beneath each was a raised dais, the east for the Hustings Court and the west for the Sherriff's Court. Small doors led to corner turrets. Another door led to the room above the Porch. The architecture of the Great Hall is discussed in greater detail in Chapter 5.

Lord Mayor Richard Whittington died in 1423 and his will paid for some of the paving – of Purbeck marble – and some of the window glazing. Other individuals donated money as well and when this ran out the City imposed surtaxes which lasted for about six years. Later a tax was levied on imported goods sold by foreigners. Foreigners did not mean people from other countries but meant traders who were not Londoners – for example, someone from Canterbury.

East Crypt, late nineteenth century.

Chapter 2

Agincourt to the Second World War

England's winning streak of military victories continued during the first decades of the Hundred Years War against France. Following Guildhall banquets celebrating King Edward III's victories at Crécy and Poitiers (1356) a similar banquet was supposedly held in 1420 to honour King Henry V, although well after the Battle of Agincourt (1415).

This may have been the first major event in the new Great Hall, as the roof had not been completed until 1418. The renowned former (and future) Lord Mayor of London Richard Whittington hosted the banquet.

Whittington had lent King Henry V large sums of money to help fund the war and naturally enough the King was most grateful, allegedly announcing to Whittington and the merry gathering, 'Happy is the King to have such a subject,' to which Whittington is said to have replied, 'No Sire, happy is the subject to have such a King.' It's said that Whittington then threw all of the King's bonds of debt into the Great Hall's burning fire. Whatever the truth of this story, the City always responded well to military victories. It was not only good for England, but trade too, from which merchants like Whittington saw many opportunities to profit.

Richard Whittington.

In September 2015 the Great Hall hosted the 600th Anniversary Banquet to mark the victory at Agincourt. The main course was Lancashire grass-fed beef, served with Dauphinoise potatoes.

In 1450 the new Guildhall was to witness the first of its many trials. This was not, however, an official trial. A rebellion, led by Jack Cade 'The Captain of Kent', had temporarily seized control of London and it seems Guildhall was commandeered as the rebel's headquarters.

The cause of the rebellion was initially to challenge corruption by those surrounding the weak and ineffectual monarch, King Henry VI. The rebels were a mixture of peasants, artisan workers and even members of Parliament. Cade himself seems to have stood for what might now be described as egalitarian views, all laid out in his manifesto, 'The Complaint of the Poor Commons of Kent'.

Marching in from Sussex and Kent and eventually mustering on Blackheath, Cade and his 5,000 followers crossed London Bridge on 3 July and entered the City. After occupying Guildhall the rebels 'arrested' James Fiennes, the Lord High Treasurer, and put him on trial for treason in the Great Hall. He was inevitably found guilty and then beheaded in front of the crowds who'd gathered in Cheapside.

Despite their supposed good intentions many of the rebels then took to looting and theft. Cade was losing control, and Londoners, some of whom had been sympathetic, turned against the rebels. When Cade returned over the river to Southwark for a night's rest the citizens closed London Bridge. On 8 July Cade and his troops attempted to re-enter the City. London's citizens fought back. Cade lost over 200 men and withdrew. London had won the Battle of London Bridge.

Jack Cade's Rebellion was over and Cade himself was killed resisting arrest in Kent. His body was bought back to London, where it was symbolically beheaded, quartered and then dragged through the streets.

King Henry V (1413-22).

Jack Cade had allegedly been a supporter of Richard, Duke of York, claimant to the throne of England during the early stages of the Wars of the Roses. Elements within the City had supported York too, which may explain their partial enthusiasm for the rebellion. The Yorkist King Edward IV later found he had many supporters in Guildhall. But of his usurper brother Richard III the Duke of Buckingham reported of the City, 'they say mum, not a word.'

Jack Cade.

Guildhall was a space unlike any other in England. During state or London ceremonials it was the one place where the high and mighty could mix purely for entertainment. They mixed without the need to swear loyalty to the hosts or indeed anyone else in the room, except to the monarch if he happened to be present.

The Great Hall was not under the ownership of the Crown, the barons or the aristocracy. Nor was it controlled by any one political elite or party. It became the ultimate common space for London government, national celebration, royal pageantry, diplomatic schmoozing, patriotic symbolism, rough justice, Machiavellian manoeuvring and commercial lobbying. In 1505 the former Lord Mayor Sir John Alwin bequeathed in his will the sum of £73 to purchase tapestries for display on Guildhall 'gaudy days' (from latin *gaudium* or merry-making).

The Lord Mayor's Banquet of 1529 is a good example of when Alwin's tapestries might have decorated a banquet. The guest list reads like a who's who of the great and powerful. Lord Chancellor Sir Thomas More, Treasurer the Duke of Suffolk, Marshall of England the Duke of Norfolk and Sir Thomas Boleyn, the father of England's future Queen Anne, were all present.

This was the way the City liked it. Politics, trade, wealth, influence, all converged at Guildhall events, which the City hosted and revelled in. The well connected sought a seat at the City table and the City was perfectly happy to oblige those it thought could help oil the wheels of City enterprise. Guildhall was only too pleased to honour those it felt advanced City and national prosperity.

Investment took many forms and the City was well prepared to help fund the national effort and promote wider prosperity. In April 1588 the Court of Common Council voted to equip and arm sixteen of the largest and best merchant ships on the Thames, in preparation for the expected Spanish Armada. Financial assistance was also given to Sir Walter Raleigh and the Virginia Company colonies in the New World.

10

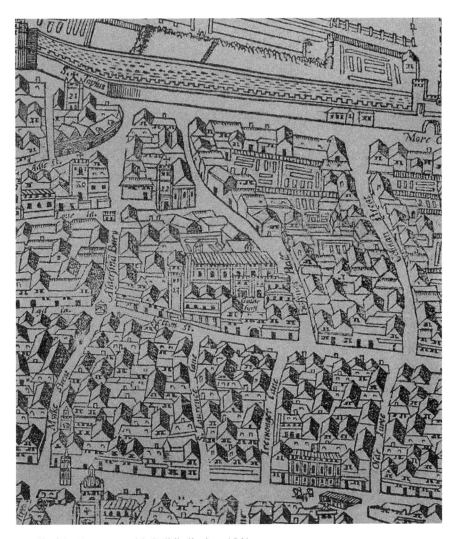

Detail of the Agas map with Guildhall, circa 1561.

On one occasion though, monarchy came calling and made the City an offer it couldn't refuse. King James I had decided to colonise Ulster with what came to be called, as in the New World, plantations. Following the Nine Years War to subjugate Ireland (1594-1603) it was decided to colonise Ulster with Britons, mainly as a way to prevent fresh outbreaks of rebellion against the Crown. Population movement between Scotland and Ireland was nothing new, but these plantations were a concerted effort to send over English and Scottish Protestants to settle empty or emptied farmland. The plantations would mainly be settled around garrisons or new towns such as Londonderry.

Badge of the Honourable Irish Society on the old office in Guildhall Buildings.

The new landowners were called Undertakers. They were often wealthy landowners from mainland Britain who would send over existing tenants to boost numbers. Veterans of the Nine Years War were also granted land, and this is where James I required City money.

He asked the most powerful Guilds in the City to fund both the purchase of land for the veterans and the building of Londonderry and Coleraine. Reluctantly the City agreed and thus was formed the Honourable Irish Society. The old Irish Chamber still stands on the south-east corner of Guildhall Yard, two small shields clearly visible combining the City emblem with the red hand of Ulster.

> The Guilds had divested most of their property investments by the nineteenth century. However, the Irish Society still owns some rights in Ulster, such as the walls of Derry which are a tourist attraction, and fishing licenses on the River Bann. Income derived from these interests is given to charity.

The English Civil War split loyalties in the City, as much as anywhere else in the kingdom. King Charles I, at first maintaining his support, attended a banquet at Guildhall in November 1641 where he knighted the Lord Mayor, both Sheriffs, and the Recorder of the City.

Three months later, in February 1642, the King returned, searching for five members of Parliament he suspected of colluding with Scottish rebels. They had already fled Parliament, and the King, having announced in the Chamber of the House of Commons that 'the birds have flown', now believed they might be 'lurking in the City'. He attended the Court of Common Council where members divided, competing with cries of 'Parliament, privileges of Parliament' and 'God save the King'. His search for the rebels here was equally unsuccessful.

During the Civil War the City supported Parliament and a grateful Oliver Cromwell attended Court of Common Council. He gave thanks to the City for helping to pay for arms and recruit troops. But when funds were not so forthcoming later in the war he had the Lord Mayor, John Gayer, imprisoned in the Tower of London. Gayer was fined without trial and released, but Cromwell eventually recognised the dangers of City resistance and their power.

King Charles I (1625-49).

By 1660 the City had turned against the Commonwealth and supported the restoration of the monarchy. King Charles II was soon dining with the Lord Mayor and enjoying 'a welcome cupp according to the usual custome'.

The Great Plague hit London like a deathly scourge in 1665, killing around one quarter of its citizens, perhaps up to 100,000 people. And no sooner had the City survived one calamity than on 2 September 1666 another unpredicted disaster destroyed eighty per cent of the built fabric of the City of London.

The Great Fire of London killed very few. What was destroyed during the four-day fire storm was London itself. It's estimated that, within the square mile of the City, over thirteen thousand houses were burned to the ground, eighty-seven churches, old St Paul's Cathedral and forty-four Livery Halls (crucial to City trade and commerce).

Guildhall's neighbouring church of St Lawrence Jewry was no more. Fortunately the fire had not totally consumed the Great Hall. But, as Samuel Pepys recorded, 'the horrid, malicious, bloody flame' had destroyed the Guildhall roof.

A much less grand roof was built as a replacement. It was not vaulted or stone but a flat wooden construction which wouldn't be replaced until the nineteenth century.

The Great Hall today is decorated in most of its bays and niches with sculptures and displays. These tend to date from the late eighteenth century, but they are not the first art works to have been displayed in the Great Hall. To resolve post-Fire boundary and property issues the 'Fire of London Disputes Act' appointed twenty-two 'fire judges' to settle all disputes arising between tenants and landlords of burnt buildings. Specially commissioned portraits of the twenty-two fire judges used to hang in the Great Hall, until the bombing of 1940. One of

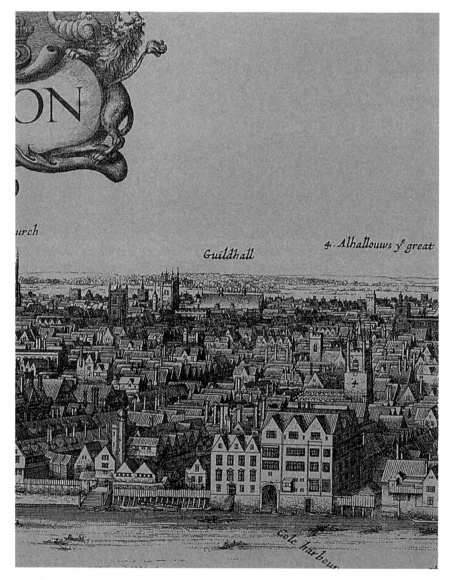

Detail of the Wenceslaus Hollar engraving of the City with Guildhall, 1647

the only portraits to survive, that of Sir Hugh Wyndham, hangs in the Guildhall Art Gallery.

Despite the initial cordiality, by the end of King Charles II's reign the City and Crown were in dispute over money, power and religion. As a display of power Charles II issued a 'Quo Warranto' in 1682, suspending the City's Charter and seizing its revenue. This Royal decree was continued by King Charles's brother, King James II, in 1685. No Lord Mayors or Aldermen were elected for six years.

The Great Fire of London. Circa late 1660s - '80s. Henry Waggoner (d.1708). Permission of Guildhall Art Gallery.

Even before the 'Quo Warranto' Charles II had a reputation for suppressing perceived opposition. On 29 December 1675 the King issued a proclamation revoking the licenses of all coffee houses. The drink may still have been regarded as a fad by some, but the coffee houses were considered to be hives of opposition to royal absolutism.

They had developed in the City from 1652 where Pasqua Rosée, the first London coffee house, was barely five streets away from Guildhall. Developing as centre's of trade, debate, gossip and disseminators of political pamphlets, their 'coffee house philosophies' were deemed, by the Crown, to promote sedition and rebellion.

King Charles II (1660-85).

The specific accusation was that coffee houses disturbed the peace and quiet of the realm, attracted the idle and disaffected and were the source of false, malicious and scandalous rumour.

On 8 January 1676 the proclamation was withdrawn. It's said that several of the King's ministers and advisors were coffee house habitues themselves. In place of a ban the coffee house proprietors had to swear an Oath of Allegiance to the Crown. By the early 1700s it's estimated there were over 550 coffee houses in London.

King William III (1688-1702).

Politics, and again religion, would soon intervene and the situation was destined to end in a most dramatic way. In April 1688 several lords came to Guildhall from Parliament and announced, to the Court of Aldermen, the flight of the Roman Catholic King James II into exile. His Protestant son-in-law William, Prince of Orange, had already landed with an army on the south coast. A declaration by the City was hastily drawn up to help William by 'maintaining the religion, the rights, the liberties that had been invaded by Jesuitical Counsels'. The Court of Common Council then sought William's protection.

The City had played its part in the 'Glorious Revolution' and within months they would entertain their saviour, now King William III, at the next Lord Mayor's Day. By 1689 the City's Charter and privileges had been restored.

The City was never shy of being in dispute with the Crown if it thought its mercantile interests were being neglected or challenged. The late eighteenth century was a time of ascendant political power, and writ large in the annals of the City is the 'Remonstrance' by Lord Mayor William Beckford aimed squarely at King George III.

The Court of Common Council was seen to have inclinations in favour of the Whig party in Parliament. While certainly pro-Royal, the Whigs were more reformist and they tended to support the supremacy of Parliament over the power of the King; and King George III became involved in the biggest parliamentary story of the day.

John Wilkes, a Member of Parliament, Alderman of the City of London, journalist, and political radical, was banned from Parliament for breaking parliamentary regulations and therefore technically being an outlaw – he had previously been jailed for obscene libel and seditious libel. Wilkes had also often written against George III's political bias, causing the King to become embroiled in this latest twist in Wilkes' life.

William Beckford was an ardent supporter of Wilkes. On Wilkes's release from prison Beckford had displayed banners outside his house with the word 'Liberty' emblazoned in letters three feet high. In May 1770 Beckford delivered his speech, or 'Remonstrance', before the King. Shocking in itself was the break with protocol in criticizing the King in public.

Memorial to William Beckford, Guildhall. Engraving 1772.

The speech nowadays seems quite mild. But it's the last lines of the 'Remonstrance' that are most cutting and a reminder of the fragility of monarchy. Beckford was reaffirming his personal loyalty to the Crown, but he also emphasised that whoever dared to insinuate that the City of London was not loyal was 'a Violator of the public's Peace, and a Betrayer of our happy constitution as it was established in the Glorious Revolution'.

That calculated reminder of the 'Glorious Revolution' of 1688, and by implication the City's support for the overthrow of King James II, must have shocked the sensibilities of the King and his supporters. Beckford's friend and political ally William Pitt the Elder exclaimed, 'the spirit of old England spoke that never-to-be-forgotten day,' and when Beckford died of a cold a few months later the City commissioned a statue of him, which to this day is still displayed in the Great Hall.

Wilkes Street, London E1, is named after John Wilkes, who gained much support from the silk weavers of Spitalfields. Wilkes became Lord Mayor in 1774. He was also a multiple duellist and, despite being referred to as 'the ugliest man in England', a notorious womaniser.

Statue of John Wilkes, Fetter Lane, EC4.

The war against the rebels in the American colonies in the eighteenth century drew support amongst the population. Not so in the City.

In the build up to the American War of Independence the Court of Common Council supported the colonists and it warned against the 'fatal policy pursued by the King's Ministers' as they 'alarm a free and commercial people'. Common Council even petitioned King George III to suspend hostilities and 'adopt conciliatory measures as might restore union, confidence and peace'.

Favourite of the City, William Pitt the Elder gave his final rousing speech in the House of Lords in 1778, about the war. Pitt had been much in favour of reaching an accommodation with the colonies, foreseeing disaster if war was fought and telling the Lords, 'And so it proved! And so it proved!'

William Pitt the Elder.

Yet Pitt also personified the internal conflict within the British establishment that regretted any diminishing of the Empire, which must be maintained at all cost, saying, 'if it is absolutely necessary to declare either for peace or war, and the former cannot be preserved with honour, why is not the latter commenced without delay? My Lords any state is better than despair. Let us at least make one effort, and if we must fall, let us fall like men!'

Pitt indeed fell, collapsing into his seat from his exertions. He died three weeks later and a grateful City commissioned the memorial to the Earl of Chatham (his official title) that we see today in the Great Hall.

War with the Americans, once ended, led into war with the French. This was a generational war that was to last over twenty years, ending only with victory over Napoleon Bonaparte at Waterloo in June 1815.

Towards the end of the Napoleonic War, Guildhall held not one but two victory banquets, albeit slightly prematurely. Both banquets were held in the summer of 1814, after Bonaparte had been exiled to Elba but before his escape to France. Nevertheless, we see a guest list which typified a Great Hall event. Present were George, the Prince Regent; the Czar of Russia; the King of Prussia; and the restored Bourbon King of France himself, Louis XVIII.

A second banquet for the Duke of Wellington was given a few weeks later. But Bonaparte did escape and did gather his troops one more time – only to lose once more to Wellington at the Battle of Waterloo.

Above: Allies Victory Banquet, 1814.

Left: Battle of Waterloo 150th Anniversary Banquet menu, 1965.

This pattern of Great Hall banquets continued in the same vein through the nineteenth century and into the twentieth. The City was occupying a comfortable niche. It was at the centre of the economic powerhouse of Empire. Trade around the Empire was free and unfettered. City money financed expansion, its insurance protected investment, and its shipping encompassed the globe. The aspirations of Parliament and the City mirrored one another and they shared in the spoils of success.

Always involved in politics, the City was a great supporter of Parliamentary reform and extension of the vote. It gladly threw a political victory banquet for Whig Prime Minister Lord Grey, whose Great Reform Act of 1832 answered those City desires.

As well as Coronation banquets many foreign monarchs and dignitaries were entertained. During the latter half of the nineteenth century the City hosted Abdul Aziz, the Sultan of Turkey; the Shah of Persia; the Czar of Russia; the King of the Hellenes (Greece); and Italian nationalist Giuseppe Garibaldi.

Lord Chancellor, the First Earl Cairns, addressing a Lord Mayor during the 1870s exclaimed, 'My Lord, you have been called upon to preside over a municipality, the grandest, the most dignified, the most opulent in the world. It is looked up to at home, and it is respected abroad.'

Without breaking step Guildhall doffed its hat at the compliment and carried on. At the Golden Jubilee Banquet for Queen Victoria in 1897 the guest list ran to 5,000 people. Honoured guests included the Kings of Belgium, Denmark, Saxony, The Hellenes, the entire British royal family and ambassadors and ministers from almost every country.

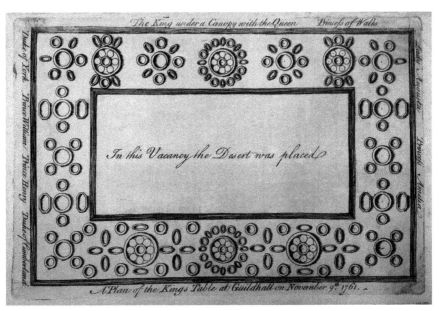

King George III. Coronation Banquet table plan, 1761

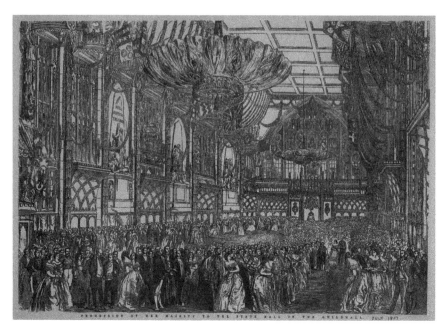

State Ball, 1851. Queen Victoria and Prince Albert to the right.

The Garibaldi biscuit is named after Giuseppe Garibaldi and was first made at the Peek Frean biscuit factory in Bermondsey, London in 1861. Garibaldi's grandson, Giuseppe 'Peppino' Garibaldi II volunteered to fight for the British in the Second Boer War in South Africa. His grandfather had been presented with a sword by the workers of Tyneside during a visit in 1854 which Peppino carried with him to war.

The twentieth century began on a military footing when the Great Hall was used by the Lord Mayor to enrol troops to serve in the Second Boer War. Fifteen hundred men signed up into what became known as the City Imperial Volunteers. The City purchased supplies and equipment for the war effort, all stored before shipment in the Great Hall.

The City played its part in ensuring the peace too, and in 1903 following the Entente Cordiale with France held a banquet to honour the visiting French President Émile Loubet. In fact banquets were very much the order of the day, as every visiting head of state and monarch would be banqueted at Guildhall. Many visited Britain in the first decade of the new century.

The Kings of Italy, Spain, Portugal, Denmark, Norway and the Hellenes were all entertained in the Great Hall, as was the King's cousin, Kaiser Wilhelm II of Germany in 1907. The City once again rolled out the red carpet in 1909, and honoured the Municipality of Berlin.

Within six years Britain was at war with Germany and, on 5 September 1914, a few days after war had been declared, Prime Minister Herbert Asquith addressed a meeting in the Great Hall affirming Britain's just cause, and confidence.

Above: King Edward VII. Coronation Banquet invitation, 1902.

Below: *The City Imperial Volunteers in the Guildhall, 1900*. John Bacon, 1902.
Permission of Guildhall Art Gallery.

It would not be until after the First World War had ended that another visiting head of state would be welcomed by the City. In December 1918 American President Woodrow Wilson addressed the Court of Common Council in the Great Hall.

President Loubet in Guildhall 1903.

One could say that it was business as usual during the inter-war years. Banquets were held for the new monarch King George VI and visiting heads of state, some reflecting the new post-First World War accommodation. The Kings of Belgium, Romania and Italy were entertained, as was French President Gaston Doumergue. New names appeared as well. The City welcomed King Faud I of Egypt, King Feisal of Iraq and King Amanullah of Afghanistan.

Celebrations would come to an abrupt halt during the Second World War. As much as the nation could prepare and perhaps even foresee some destruction on the home front, the extent of the oncoming blitzkrieg could only be guessed at. Guildhall, like much of London, would suffer extensive damage.

Prime Minister H.H. Asquith addressing the crowd in Guildhall, 1914.

Chapter 3

The Great Hall: Sculptures and Displays

Gog & Magog – The Guildhall Giants

Sculptor: David Evans, 1953.
Limewood and gold leaf: 9' high.

Mythical guardians of London. The origins of Gog and Magog are shrouded in mystery. These Great Hall representations were impressively carved to replace the eighteenth-century giants, destroyed during the Blitz when the Great Hall was seriously bomb damaged.

Gog.

Magog.

Gog stands to the right holding a 'morning star' spiked ball in one hand with sword and dagger to his left. A quiver of arrows is visible on his back. Magog stands to the left, holding a halberd of a pike and axe in his right hand while gripping a shield with the phoenix emblazoned on it in his left. The phoenix is symbolic of London's resurgence after the Second World War. Evans copied Magog's post-Great Fire shield which also featured a phoenix, symbolic then of London's resurrection after the Great Fire of 1666.

Both figures are Romano-British in attire, clearly warriors and harking back to the days of King Arthur. Gog and Magog were both mentioned in Geoffrey of Monmouth's fantastical *History of the Kings of Britain*, a twelfth-century story book from which many of our King Arthur myths originate. Gog and Magog though are placed by Monmouth within a pre-Roman Britain. Once called Gogmagog and Corineus, they were guardians of the 'New Troy' we call London. Corineus becomes lost in the fog of London and they re-emerge centuries later as Gog and Magog.

Linked forever with the City of London, effigies of the giants have been part of the Lord Mayor's Show since the sixteenth century. Portable versions of the Guildhall Giants are made of wicker and stored in a secret cupboard. They emerge every November to take their place in the parade.

Gog and Magog. By the Basketmakers Company.

The West Windows

The great perpendicular West Windows were formerly called the Prince Consort Memorial Windows. Destroyed during the Blitz in 1940, the new windows were manufactured to a design by Giles Gilbert Scott during his post-war refurbishment.

Each window contains the names of previous Lord Mayors above a chevron and monogram of the reigning monarch under which they served. The design continues around the upper clerestory windows (clockwise) returning to the West Window with up to date details of the most recent Lord Mayor.

At the window pinnacle is a St George Cross and Sword of St Paul (patron saint of the City of London). Significant window segments include:

1189: Henry Fitzailwyn, London's first named Mayor is shown on the left window, with King Richard I, the Lion Heart.

1215: King John, below King Richard I. London's citizens were given the right to elect their own mayor in a charter granted by King John to the City of London in 1215. Weeks later the Magna Carta decreed the City could retain all its ancient liberties. William Hardel, Mayor at the time, was a signatory to Magna Carta, but is not represented here.

Richard 'Dick' Whittington and King Henry IV are visible to the right. Whittington was Lord Mayor four times, in 1397, 1397-8, 1406-7 and 1419-20 and served as Lord Mayor under three Monarchs: Richard II, Henry IV and Henry V.

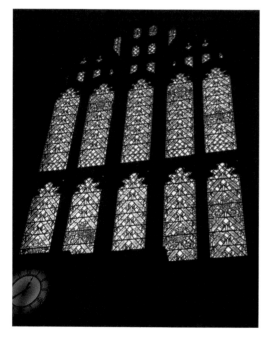

The central panel of the West Window.

28

Sir Winston Churchill (1874-1965)

Sculptor: Oscar Nemon, 1955.
Bronze with Portland stone base: 4'6" high x 4' wide

Before this statue was commissioned by the Corporation of the City of London, Churchill had already been made an honorary freeman of the City of London. During 1943 and within the bomb-damaged, temporarily-roofed Great Hall, Churchill was awarded his scroll containing the Freedom of the City. It was presented in a small oak case made from timbers retrieved from the debris of the roof.

Nemon became a friend of Churchill and, applying some creativity as well as humour, Churchill's face is supposed to show a bull dog look from the left and a wry smile from the right. Churchill's wife Clementine said, 'Your bust represents my husband as I see him and think of him.'

The extended left leg also has a rubbed shiny foot, just like his statue in the Houses of Parliament (also by Nemon). It is tradition for a Member of Parliament to rub the left foot of Churchill's statue in the Members' Lobby for luck, especially if about to deliver a difficult speech.

Sir Winston Churchill.

Churchill's titles at the time of being sculpted are abbreviated on the base: KG – Knight of the Order of the Garter; OM – Order of Merit; CH – Companion of Honour and MP – Member of Parliament.

Oscar Nemon (née Neuman 1906-85) was a Jewish refugee from Nazi-occupied Europe. Already a successful sculptor he had lived with the artist René Magritte in Brussels and was the only person to sculpt Sigmund Freud. Churchill himself was a talented artist, although the only sculpture he ever completed was a bust of his friend Nemon.

Monument to Horatio Nelson (1758-1805)

Sculptor: James Smith, 1811.
Marble: 24' high x 14' wide

The first thing one observes is that Nelson, the hero of the Battle of Trafalgar, is barely represented. Nelson's death at the battle, in October 1805, rendered him absent in person from the nation's celebrations. An absence painfully felt is symbolised in this giant, bombastic, marble sculpture.

Horatio Nelson.

The unknown James Smith won the commission for this important and prestigious memorial by submitting the cheapest estimate. It projects a strong image of Empire as well as that of a nation in mourning.

The entire edifice is resplendent with maritime symbolism. Neptune with his trident is reclining on a dolphin. Britannia is seated on a mourning lion, looking downcast at a small medallion portrait of Nelson. A crowned female figure with her back to us (hiding her tears?) represents the City of London. She is engraving three of Nelson's naval victories onto a stone monument: The Nile, Copenhagen and Trafalgar. All are balanced on a rocky base covered in seaweed and shells and surrounded by ships rope, cannon and heavy, swagged flags.

The marble base displays a scene from the Battle of Trafalgar with some excellent small details, such as cannon shot from British ships piercing the sails of the French fleet. Nelson's flagship *Victory* is seen breaking the French lines just to left of the centre. Around the base, two sailors flank the central frieze in small niches. One holds ropes and weights used in navigation. The other is holding a ramrod and plug, used with naval cannon. The sonorous tribute is written by the playwright Richard Brinsley Sheridan.

The statue was damaged during the Blitz, with the head of Neptune being destroyed. Today we see a post-war replacement of Neptune's head.

Monument to the Duke of Wellington (1769-1852)

Sculptor: John Bell, 1857.
Marble: 27' 6" high x 14' wide

This is another statue replete with symbolism and allegory. The Duke of Wellington was a remarkable man whose long career encompassed military commander, victor at the Battle of Waterloo and Prime Minister.

The Iron Duke himself stands proud in the centre. He is wearing a military cloak, the Star of the Bath (Order of the Bath), the Ribbon of the Garter (Order of the Garter) and the Waterloo Medal. In his left hand he is holding a field marshal's baton and in his right hand a scroll (the Peace of 1815). Wellington is clearly a Very Important Person. At his feet his tribute, wreathed in laurel, is plain speaking, blunt and to the point (allegedly much like Wellington himself): Wisdom. Duty. Honour.

There had been no new memorials in the Great Hall for almost half a century and this was a prestigious commission. Bell was a well-known sculptor who went on to create the Crimean War Memorial, appropriately in Waterloo Place, London SW1.

Seated to Wellington's right is Peace, holding corn and a wreath of oak, to symbolise prosperity. They seem to look into each other's eyes. To Wellington's left

The Duke of Wellington.

is War. He is clasping the victor's wreath but his sword is sheathed and he's looking a little redundant. Following Wellington's victory at Waterloo in 1815 there would be no pan-European war until 1914.

Carved into the right-hand panel of the marble base is the Duke of Wellington's crest of a lion's head and the motto '*Virtutis Fortuna Comes*', or 'Fortune Favours the Brave'. On the left panel is a dove holding an olive branch with the inscription '*Pacis Imponere Morem*', or 'To Impose Peace'.

The central panel of the marble base features the dramatic relief *Last Charge of Waterloo*. This epic battle in June 1815 was the decisive victory over Napoleon and by all accounts a bloody and vicious encounter. The allied army (British, Dutch and Prussian) numbered 118,000. The French army was outnumbered standing at 73,000. By the day's end the Allies had lost 17,000 dead or wounded. The French suffered 25,000 dead or wounded plus 8,000 captured.

British troops can be seen to the left in the frieze, face to face with the French, in mortal combat. The Duke of Wellington is visible on his horse Copenhagen, hat raised in salute or perhaps encouragement (possibly even shouting 'up and at them!'). To the top right on a distant hill is Bonaparte, all but vanquished, a mere spectator. He is seated on his own faithful horse Marengo.

Following Waterloo Bonaparte lived out his days on the south Atlantic island of St Helena, dying in 1821. His horse Marengo, on the other hand, was bought back to England and died at the ripe old age of 38 in 1831. His skeleton is sometimes on display at the National Army Museum in Chelsea, London SW3.

Monument to William Pitt, Earl of Chatham (1708-78)

Sculptor: John Bacon the Elder, 1782.
Marble: 24' 6" high x 14' wide

Every figure, allegory and detail on this statue is symbolic of the status of Chatham and also of the greatness of Great Britain. Politician and Prime Minister, William Pitt the Elder was recognised as one of the propounders of Empire. This was a time when Great Britain ruled the seas and her colonies were developing into dominions.

William Pitt the Elder.

Pitt, standing central and on high, is dressed as a Roman senator. His oratorical skills were legendary and he represents a Britain on the cusp of controlling the greatest empire since Rome. His left hand rests on the rudder of government. With his right arm he is embracing Commerce; she holds a compass. The City of London, represented by wearing a London Wall-like mural crown, has her back to us and is reaching out to Commerce. The beehive at her feet symbolises Industry. Britannia, relaxed and at ease, is seated on a contented lion. Draped across her knees a mythical cornucopia overflows, symbolising trade and plenty. Four infants can also be seen, each representing one of the four corners of the globe: Europe, Africa, India and America. In case you were still not able to understand the message, the entire grouping is seated upon and around maritime symbols of sail, rope and an anchor. Britain's sea-bound trade is protected by the use of cannon and cannonball, visible to the right.

The City of London loved Pitt the Elder. He was their 'horn of plenty', their supporter and enabler during a time of expanding overseas trade and nascent Empire. This was their tribute, in marble and overblown prose written in the panel below the statue. Beneath the tribute is an oval medallion with the cap of Liberty and the inscription 'Libertas'.

> Like the memorial to Nelson this statue suffered damage during the Blitz and looks a little un-buffed and dull. Parts of the upper half are a plaster replacement.

Monument to William Pitt the Younger (1759-1806)

Sculptor: James Bubb, 1813.
Marble: 23' high x 14' wide

Pitt the Younger was a younger son of Chatham and is most well known for being prime minister at the age of 24. He was prime minister almost continuously from 1783 until his early death aged 46. Great Britain had just lost the American colonies and would soon be fighting the French in a long and arduous multi-generational war. The nation's finances were in need of efficient management.

To help support the war economy Pitt introduced income tax, a measure intended to be temporary. It's said that by his death Pitt was worn down by the pressures of state. He had suffered from gout since childhood, was a heavy drinker and something of a gambler. He died owing £40,000 and a grateful government settled his debts with his creditors.

Like his father, Pitt the Younger stands atop his memorial. He is wearing his Chancellor of the Exchequer robes and is gesturing as if giving a speech. To his right is Apollo symbolising wisdom and learning. Mercury stands to Pitt's left holding a scroll and caduceus wand. Mercury represents Commerce, but he was also guide to

William Pitt the Younger.

the dead and protector of, amongst others, gamblers. A triumphant Britannia is riding a mythical hippocampus (sea horse), with trident and fish in hand. She had originally held a bolt of lightning in her right hand (to hurl at Britain's enemies) but this was destroyed during the Blitz. Why is the replacement a fish? No one is entirely sure. The maritime symbolism is clear enough though. The British navy had destroyed Bonaparte's navy at the Battle of Trafalgar in 1805. Britannia, wearing a helmet designed like a ship's prow, metaphorically and literally rules the waves.

James Bubb was an unusual choice as sculptor. A relative unknown, he tendered the lowest bid of £3,400. Bubb worked mainly at the Coade Stone Manufactory in nearby Lambeth, sculpting architectural decoration and ornaments. Coade Stone was a woman-made composite stone perfected by Eleanor Coade in the late 1700s. Used in many buildings, including Buckingham Palace, its most visible surviving example can be seen in the South Bank Lion on the south-east corner of Westminster Bridge.

The *hippocampi* are the memory components of the human brain and are shaped like a sea horse. It's been shown that London 'black cab' taxi drivers have enlarged hippocampi, as they train for at least three years memorising London's streets and buildings in a process called 'the Knowledge'. During this learning process their long term memory and spatial memory increases so much that the hippocampi grow.

Monument to William Beckford (1709-70)

Sculptor: John Francis Moore, 1772.
Marble: 18' high x 11' wide

This statue of a hectoring, well-dressed gentleman caught in mid-oratorical flow is the oldest in the Great Hall. Not a national figure, Beckford was however a City man through and through and was honoured as such in life and death. The chain

William Beckford.

of office of Lord Mayor hangs around Beckford's neck. He became Lord Mayor in 1762 and 1769, dying in office.

He was the son of a Jamaican plantation and slave owner, sent to England for his education and to further the family interests. At this he was very successful, and in pursuing his own political career. One of the wealthiest men in the country, Beckford's banquets and favours became legendary. He became Member of Parliament for Shaftesbury and then the City of London itself and regarded himself as something of a political liberal.

Beckford was a Whig and supported the supremacy of Parliament and a constitutional monarchy. This statue celebrates the event for which the City remembers him most, the so called 'Remonstrance' (mentioned in Chapter 2). Beckford broke with protocol by challenging the view of King George III, in public, about alleged Royal interference in an issue of political corruption (the Wilkes exclusion).

The statue features Beckford in mid-Remonstrance. His words are inscribed on the black marble tablet below. To our left is a figure of The City, forlorn, wearing the Cap of Maintenance and holding the City shield. On our right is a drooping female figure representing Trade and Navigation. She wears the mural crown and holds an anchor. A very small cornucopia sits upon a compass.

The City was feeling quite threatened at this point, having recently come through war with the French and the American colonies becoming restless. Beckford was considered to have nobly stood up for the mercantile classes and the interests of the City of London.

> Such was Beckford's influence he wrote a letter in 1758 to Pitt the Elder proposing the attack on French Martinique: 'the negroes and stock of the island are worth above £4m... for God's sake attempt the capture without delay.' Despite his fame and liberal disposition, a ballad was written about him, a part of which is,
>
> *To see a slave he could not bear...*
> *Unless it were his own.*
>
> Beckford was not above pomposity, nor having his pomposity pricked.

The Buffet

The oak wood panelled canopy on the south side of the Great Hall is known as The Buffet. To English speakers nowadays this often refers to an unseated meal served on a counter, but its original meaning referred to the table or serving bench itself.

Originally the Dais at the east end of the Great Hall was used for the top table only when the monarch was in attendance. Today either the Dais or

Buffet is used as the top table for banquets. As with the wooden galleries and timber panelling the Buffet is part of Giles Gilbert Scott's post-Second World War renovations. The Gothic styling is to his design and carved by the firm of Maple-Martyn (formerly a part of Maples) based on the 1891 original. Dragons, symbols of the City of London, surmount the canopy. Their hands are clasped in order to hold banners. Niches within the Buffet are left empty for most of the time but are filled with Lord Mayoral plate and ornaments when the Lord Mayor attends a banquet. There are also rest places (brackets) for the Lord Mayor's official sword and mace. The coats of arms represent the Sheriffs and Chief Commoners from 1891.

The Buffet.

Mikhail Gorbachev
speaking from the
Buffet in April 1989.

Royal Fusiliers (City of London Regiment) South African War Memorial

Sculptor: Frederick William Pomeroy, 1907.
Bronze: 9' 10" high x 7' 2" wide

This is a memorial to the local men who fought in the Second Boer War (1899-1902). Guildhall had itself been a recruiting station and in January 1900 thirteen hundred men signed up. The Royal Regiment of Fusiliers was an infantry regiment originally formed in 1685 during the reign of King James II. Their headquarters had always been within the Tower of London.

The memorial consists of three bronze relief panels set into blind gothic tracery. There is another bronze panel at the base with the City shield. General opinion was that as a work of art it 'harmonizes excellently with the ancient character of the masonry around.' This is a modern memorial but like earlier Great Hall statues replete with symbolism.

Royal Fusiliers
Memorial.

The central panel contains a list of the dead. The insignia of the Order of the Garter sits on top. In each of the side panels is a small relief of Medusa's head (death) above a leaping horse (vitality). The female figure in the left panel represents Victory holding the palm of martyrdom. The panel on the right is especially interesting. It depicts an ordinary trooper in mourning for his comrades. His hands are resting, almost in prayer, on the stock of his downturned rifle. A British soldier is for the first time wearing a khaki uniform.

This gesture to the common soldier was not consistent, unfortunately. Following the memorial's unveiling the Lord Mayor threw a lavish lunch at Mansion House, for the officers of the Regiment only.

At the time of the Regiment's foundation in the late seventeenth century the fusil was the most up-to-date flintlock musket. It was a light rifle with a long barrel. It's said that the sight of unfit recruits during the Boer War led to Robert Baden Powell, who served in the war, setting up the Boy Scout movement. F.W. Pomeroy's most famous work is the figure of Justice on the dome of the Central Criminal Court (the Old Bailey).

The Mayoral Window

Artist: Alfred Fisher, 1989. Glass.

The Mayoral Window was commissioned to mark the 800th anniversary of the City of London Mayoralty in 1989. It's a fine example of modern stained glass craftsmanship and was designed and made by Alfred Fisher at the Chapel Studios in Kings Langley, Hertfordshire.

The coat of arms on the top left represents Henry Fitzailwyn, first Mayor from 1189 to 1212. King John decreed that the Mayor should be selected annually and swear allegiance to the Sovereign. In return for this the City of London's rights and privileges were enshrined in Magna Carta.

To the right is the coat of arms of the City of London: the

The Mayoral Window.

shield of St George and sword of St Paul, patron saint of the City of London, supported by two heraldic dragons and the City motto 'Domine Dirige Nos' (Lord, Guide Us).

The middle section of the window depicts a highlighted story of the City since 1189. The left window focuses mainly on Henry Fitzailwyn, acknowledged as the first Mayor of the City of London. We see the diligent Fitzailwyn planning house building, welcoming King Richard I on his return from the Third Crusade and re-planning the City following its first great fire in 1212.

The right hand panel begins with Dick Whittington, cat playing at his feet, followed by the Great Fire of 1666, and Christopher Wren, architect of the new St Paul's Cathedral. After the Great Fire a new roof for the Great Hall was designed, which is also represented. The Great Hall was heavily bombed in the Blitz and this too is featured, followed by the modern resurrection of London, symbolised in a depiction of Tower 42 (originally known as the NatWest Tower) and Lloyd's of London.

Along the bottom of the window is the coat of arms of Hugh Bidwell, Lord Mayor in 1989 (the year of the window's installation) and also of the Worshipful Company of Glaziers who paid for the window to be made.

Privileged Regiments.

Privileged Regiments Coats of Arms

The Coats of Arms of the twelve regiments on display signify a certain privileged status. Each regiment has the trust of the City of London and is allowed to march through the City streets with bayonets fixed, colours or banners flying and drums beating.

It's a tradition dating from the Restoration period, during the late seventeenth century, and was partly intended to encourage recruitment. Much of the equipment and weaponry used would also have been manufactured by members of the City Livery Companies. Some of these regiments still have City connections and some are Army Reserves Regiments.

From the left the list of regiments are: The London Regiment, The Royal Marines, The Grenadier Guards, Princess of Wales's Royal Regiment, The Royal Regiment of Fusiliers, The Honourable Artillery Company, The Coldstream Guards, The Blues and Royals, The Rifles, 600 (City of London) Squadron Royal Auxiliary Air Force, London Division Royal Naval Reserve.

The Livery Banners and Frieze

In plain sight but often overlooked are the banners hanging from the high oak roof, on both sides as you walk through the Great Hall. The Great Hall has been at the centre of Guildhall life and ceremony for over 600 years. Central to the governance of the City are the Livery Companies, formerly known as the Guilds. We see on display the banners of the 'Great Twelve' guilds. Guilds are also known as Worshipful Companies because their communal activity extended to joint worship and prayer.

The status of the Great Twelve was set in 1515, based on how many times each guild had provided a Lord Mayor. The banners we see displayed, in order of precedence, are:

1. Mercers (north wall, between Wellington and Chatham Memorial).
2. Grocers.
3. Drapers.

4. Fishmongers.
5. Goldsmiths.
6. Merchant Taylors.
7. Skinners.
8. Haberdashers.
9. Salters.
10. Ironmongers.
11. Vintners
12. Clothworkers.

The Frieze behind the banners contains the motto of each Livery Company in gold gothic lettering. For the Mercers it is *Honor Deo* (Honour to God). The shields of all the other Companies are ranged above the clerestory (the top windows).

> The Skinners and Merchant Taylors disagreed about their importance and have always alternated between positions six and seven in the Great Twelve. Allegedly this is the origin of the phrase to be at 'sixes and sevens'. The dispute is said to have begun in 1484, but the Order of Precedence not set until 1515.

Mercers' Banner.

Chapter 4

The Great Hall: The Trials

On the north wall of the Great Hall to the right of the statue of the Duke of Wellington there is a plaque commemorating the trials that took place here. These trials were mostly for high treason and heresy.

The trials outlined on the plaque were held between 1546 and 1615. This was a period of political and religious upheaval in England. The established religion of the country – Roman Catholic or Protestant – could change depending on

Trials plaque in the Great Hall.

44

which monarch was ruling at the time. Religious loyalties, shifting alliances, plotting and intrigue could sometimes result in accusations of high treason, trial and execution.

Trials were held at Guildhall for two reasons. Firstly the Great Hall was large and could accommodate a lot of people. These were show trials and required a large audience. Secondly the Hall was secure and close to the Tower of London where the accused were often held. These are the people who were tried, in their order on the plaque:

Anne Askew (1521-46)

One of the most tragic was the case of Anne Askew, a 25-year-old Protestant preacher and poet. She was originally from Lincolnshire and the daughter of Sir William Askew, a knight at the court of King Henry VIII. She had married a Catholic, but he threw her out for her beliefs. She had wanted to divorce him anyway and she came to London and started preaching under her maiden name.

She was arrested for her beliefs, taken to the Tower of London and tortured, the only woman recorded to have been tortured there. She was put on the rack – a torture instrument designed to pull the victim's arms and legs apart – to force her to inform on others like herself. She refused.

She was convicted of heresy in 1546 and condemned to burn at Smithfield. This was an area close to where Smithfield Market is now and which was often used for executions. She was burned to death there with three other Protestant heretics. The rack had damaged her body so badly that she was unable to walk to the stake and had to be carried there in a chair. A chair was also lashed to the stake to which she was chained for her execution.

Henry Howard, Earl of Surrey (1516-47)

Henry Howard was from Hertfordshire, an aristocrat of royal descent – he was the grandson of the Duke of Norfolk – and in his youth became companion to one of King Henry VIII's illegitimate sons, the Duke of Richmond and Somerset. In 1524 he was given the title of Earl of Surrey and in 1533 he married the Earl of Oxford's daughter Frances de Vere. He was made a Knight of the Garter in 1541 and was regarded as a good and loyal soldier, serving as a general in Henry VIII's wars in France. He was also involved in suppressing the Pilgrimage of Grace rebellion against the dissolution of the monasteries. There was another side to him: he had a reputation for being rash and headstrong, and he was imprisoned twice in the Fleet Prison, once for breaking windows in a London street.

He was also a poet and wrote 'Satire Against the Citizens of London' as a consequence of his imprisonment. He is considered to be one of the founders of English Renaissance poetry. Along with Thomas Wyatt he was a pioneer of the sonnet verse form and was the first English poet to use unrhymed iambic pentameter, or blank verse. He and Wyatt became known as 'The Fathers of the English Sonnet'.

The Howard family had many enemies at King Henry VIII's court and there was some plotting against Henry Howard. The King became convinced that he was scheming against his son Prince Edward and wanted to take the throne from him. He had Howard imprisoned and tried for high treason and he was beheaded on Tower Hill 19 January 1547, aged 29.

Henry Howard, Earl of Surrey.

Sir Nicholas Throckmorton (1516-71)

Sir Nicholas was the son of Sir George Throckmorton and Katherine Vaux. He was brought up among the Parr family, including that of Katherine Parr who was the last of King Henry VIII's wives. In his youth he was a strong supporter of the Protestant reformation and is even said to have visited Anne Askew in prison. He became a friend of John Dudley the Duke of Northumberland, who later became regent to the young King Edward VI.

In 1545 he became Member of Parliament for Maldon and later for Devizes, Northamptonshire, Old Sarum, Lyme Regis and Tavistock. He was eventually an MP in four monarchs' reigns and was knighted in 1547. During the attempt to put Lady Jane Grey on the throne instead of Queen Mary in 1553 he found himself drawn to both sides, but ended up siding with Queen Mary.

By 1554 he was suspected of being involved in the Thomas Wyatt rebellion. This was a rebellion of Protestants who wanted to stop Queen Mary marrying the Roman Catholic King Philip II of Spain. The rebellion was unsuccessful and the ringleaders were tried and executed. Throckmorton was tried at Guildhall in 1554. The judges were against him but he managed to convince the jury of his innocence. The court responded by fining and imprisoning the jury! Throckmorton was returned to the Tower. He was released a year later and fearing he would be suspected of being involved in the Dudley Conspiracy (see below) he went to France. He was finally pardoned in 1557 and even served in Queen Mary's army.

Lady Jane Grey (1537-54) and her husband
Lord Guildford Dudley (1535-54)

Probably the most famous case to be tried in the Great Hall was that of 16-year-old Lady Jane Grey, the Nine Day Queen. Lady Jane was the great-granddaughter of King Henry VII, a young intellectual and pious Protestant. The regent at the court of the young King Edward VI (1547-53) was the staunch Protestant Duke of Northumberland. He arranged with Jane's father, the Duke of Suffolk, that Jane should marry his son Lord Guildford Dudley, though it is said she entered this marriage unwillingly.

King Edward VI was sick and dying, probably with tuberculosis. Fearing the accession of the Catholic Mary Tudor, who was the true heir, Northumberland persuaded Edward to declare his sisters, Princess Mary and Princess Elizabeth, illegitimate and to name his own daughter-in-law the Protestant Lady Jane as the next monarch. He did this and when young Edward died Lady Jane Grey was unwillingly declared Queen on 10 July 1553. She is said to have fainted when she was told. Unfortunately for her and Northumberland the country supported the true

The Execution of Lady Jane Grey, 1834. Paul Delaroche. Permission of Guildhall Art Gallery.

heir, Mary Tudor, and would not accept Lady Jane. Mary quickly raised an army and support for Northumberland evaporated.

Lady Jane and her husband Dudley were tried for high treason in the Great Hall. They were found guilty and condemned to death but the sentence was suspended. However, Jane's father became implicated in a rebellion against Queen Mary led by Sir Thomas Wyatt and as a result she and Dudley were hastily executed, she at Tower Green and he on Tower Hill. Her father was executed soon after.

Archbishop Thomas Cranmer (1489-1556)

Thomas Cranmer was Archbishop of Canterbury in the reigns of King Henry VIII, King Edward VI and Queen Mary. He was born into a family with clerical and academic leanings and he went to Jesus College Cambridge. His first wife, Joan, died in childbirth along with the child. He subsequently took holy orders in 1520.

He helped King Henry VIII with his marriage to Anne Boleyn, the annulment of his marriage to Catherine of Aragon and the consequent split with the Church of Rome. Cranmer had continually been on missions to Europe, including Germany, and he married his second wife Margaret there, demonstrating his repudiation of compulsory celibacy for priests. He became Archbishop of Canterbury as a result of the trust King Henry had placed in him, firstly over the annulment of his marriage, but also because he supported the idea that the King was in charge of the church in his kingdom. During Henry's reign he began to establish the structures of the newly formed Church of England.

Cranmer was a firm believer in the Reformation and in King Henry VIII's anti-papal cause. He was a close ally of Lord Chancellor Thomas Cromwell. Under King Henry he did not make many changes to the Church but under King Edward VI he worked on many reforms, among them the Book of Common Prayer and interpretation of the Eucharist.

Thomas Cranmer.

After the Roman Catholic Queen Mary came to the throne in 1553 he was tried at Guildhall for treason and found guilty. He said afterwards he confessed more than was true. He was then taken to Oxford and tried again, this time for heresy, with two other notable Protestant reformers, Hugh Latimer and Nicholas Ridley, who were later burned within sight of his prison window. Here he slowly made some recantations and might have been acquitted as a result but Queen Mary thought an example should be made of him and he was condemned to death. At the eleventh hour he renounced his recantations and was burned at the stake.

Henry Peckham (d.1556) and John Daniel (d.1556)

Henry Peckham and John Daniel were conspirators in a plot to stage an insurrection against Queen Mary called the Dudley Conspiracy, led by Sir Henry Dudley in 1555. The plan was to overthrow Queen Mary with armed assistance from mercenaries and Protestant exiles in France. Part of the plot involved robbing the exchequer of money to help pay for the mercenaries and ships. The conspiracy came to nothing and the conspirators were arrested. Peckham and Daniel informed on their fellow conspirators at their trial, hoping for a pardon, but were still condemned and executed at Tower Hill in 1556.

John Felton (d.1570)

John Felton was a Roman Catholic martyr. He was a wealthy man from a Norfolk family who lived in Southwark. His wife had been a maid of honour to Queen Mary. He was arrested for nailing a papal bull (a decree from the Pope) from Pope Pius V, excommunicating Queen Elizabeth I, on the gates of the Bishop of London's palace on 25 May 1570. His accomplice Lawrence Webb fled abroad.

He may have acquired the bull in Calais – although there is a theory that it came from the Spanish ambassador's chaplain. Felton gave another copy of the bull to an associate who betrayed him when searches were made of Catholic houses.

The posting of the bull on the gates was an act of treason because it excommunicated Queen Elizabeth and as a consequence would have released her subjects from their loyalty to her. There were also plenty of Catholics in Europe who might try to depose her. The bull brought a period of Protestant establishment tolerance of Catholics to an end. The appearance of the bull was partly responsible for the Ridolfi Plot in which the Duke of Norfolk conspired to depose Queen Elizabeth and replace her with Mary Queen of Scots.

Felton was arrested and confessed immediately. He was sent to Newgate Prison and while there stated and signed that Elizabeth I should not be Queen of England, which was also treasonable. He was later tortured on the rack at the

Tower of London. He was tried at Guildhall on 4 August 1570 for asserting that the Queen 'had never been true Queen of England', and hanged on 8 August in the churchyard of St Paul's Cathedral. He was cut down alive and quartered. In 1886 he was beatified by Pope Leo XIII.

Doctor Roderigo Lopez (1517-94)

Roderigo Lopez was Jewish, born in Portugal, and the son of a physician to the royal court. After studies in Coimbra, Lopez followed his father into medicine. But Judaism had been outlawed by the Inquisitions in Spain and Portugal and so in 1559 Lopez came to London. He anglicized his name to Roger and began to gain a reputation as the first and 'very skilful' house physician at St Bartholomew's Hospital.

In 1563 Lopez married Sarah Anes who came from another immigrant Portuguese family. The practice of Judaism had been outlawed in England in 1290 and both Lopez and the Anes family outwardly identified as New Christians. In secret they adhered to their Jewish faith. Secret adherents of Judaism from the Inquisitions became known as Marranos, or crypto-Jews.

In 1581 King Philip II of Spain had taken possession of the crown of Portugal and Lopez supported a Portuguese attempt to reclaim the throne, which failed. Many of these supporters subsequently switched sides and became loyal to Philip of Spain, but tensions continued.

Elizabethan engraving: 'Lopez corresponding to poison the Queen'.

Now well established in London, Lopez became physician to the Earl of Leicester and then to Queen Elizabeth I in 1581. Lopez was also physician to Francis Walsingham who was head of the English secret service – a sort of Tudor MI5 – and it was on behalf of Walsingham that Lopez became involved in the intrigues between Spain and the exiled Portuguese government.

When Walsingham died in 1590 Lopez continued to correspond with Spain on his own, and became unwillingly implicated in a plot to assassinate the Portuguese claimant Dom Antonio. His role as a court physician continued successfully too, but when treating Robert Devereux, the Earl of Essex, for a 'social disease', he foolishly broke confidence and began to gossip about the Earl's malady.

Essex was embarrassed. Through his own intelligence network he discovered the secret Spanish correspondence and began interrogating the undercover couriers. Out for revenge, Essex manipulated shady 'diplomatic' evidence and instead implicated Lopez in a plot to poison the Queen. The accusation was believed and Lopez was tried at Guildhall for high treason in 1594.

Lopez protested his innocence, but there was no Walsingham to back him up. Such was Essex's power that Walsingham's ultimate boss Robert Cecil stood back, unable to prevent the threat of torture and the signing of a false confession by Lopez.

Trial prosecutor Edward Coke accused Lopez of being 'a murderous villain and a Jewish doctor worse than Judas, not a new Christian but a very Jew'. It didn't help when it was revealed that Lopez had been covertly funding a secret synagogue in Amsterdam. Lopez was found guilty. Queen Elizabeth delayed signing his death warrant for three months and returned all of his property, which she was entitled to keep, to his family. But in June 1594 Lopez was hung, drawn and quartered at Tyburn.

Some think Lopez was the inspiration for Shakespeare's Shylock character in *The Merchant of Venice*. In 1601 Robert Devereux was himself executed for high treason.

Henry Garnet (1555-1606)

Henry Garnet, son of a Derbyshire schoolmaster, was educated at Winchester College where he was an outstanding pupil. The school thought he should go to New College, Oxford, but instead he decided to go to London where he worked as a proof-reader and corrector for Richard Tottell, who published legal works. In 1575 he journeyed to the continent where in 1582 he became ordained as a Jesuit priest.

He returned to Protestant England in 1586 and soon became the superior Jesuit priest here. Operating in secret he started a pro-Catholic secret press and increased the number of houses which could shelter priests. When King James I came to the throne in 1603 English Catholics hoped for more tolerance but it did not happen. Garnet was told to try to stop English Catholics resorting to violence because of this, but, as everyone knows, the Gunpowder Plot of 1605 went ahead anyway.

Robert Catesby, one of the Gunpowder Plotters, confessed the plot beforehand to a priest who reported it to Garnet. Garnet tried to stop the plot but failed. After the plot was discovered there was no hope of any tolerance for Catholics and many were hunted down.

Henry Garnet was arrested on 27 January 1606. He was imprisoned in the Tower of London and charged with complicity in the Gunpowder Plot. He was tried at Guildhall, found guilty and sentenced to death. It's said that King James I attended the trial incognito. Garnet was hung, drawn and quartered on 3 May 1606 in the churchyard of St. Paul's Cathedral.

Sir Gervase Helwys (1561-1615)

Jacobean intrigues were as complicated as those of the Tudors, as the following story shows. From a Nottinghamshire family, Gervase Helwys went into law and was admitted to the Middle Temple in 1579. He was knighted by King James I in 1603.

Helwys became friendly with the powerful Howard family and Henry Howard, Earl of Northampton, engineered his appointment as Lieutenant of the Tower of London in 1613 at a cost of £2,000.

Northampton wanted King James I's favourite, Robert Carr, Viscount Rochester, to marry his great niece, Frances Howard, so that the Howards would have greater influence on the King. Frances was already married to the Earl of Essex but wanted the marriage nullified so that she could marry Carr. Carr had a friend and adviser, Sir Thomas Overbury, who was against the marriage of Carr to Frances Howard and the consequential connection to the Howard family.

Overbury's enemies had him imprisoned in the Tower but ideally wanted him out of the way permanently. Under Helwys' lieutenancy one Richard Weston tried and eventually succeeded in poisoning Overbury. Helwys discovered the plot but didn't report it because he knew the Howards – who had arranged for him to have the lieutenancy – would be implicated. He did try, unsuccessfully, to disrupt the plot.

Overbury's death was not originally seen as a poisoning but two years later an investigation led to the examination and conviction of Weston for the murder. At Helwys' subsequent trial for aiding and abetting Weston the examination of and reference to correspondence from both the Howards and Helwys implicated him. He was found guilty of being an accessory 'before the fact was done' and hanged at Tower Hill in 1615.

Chapter 5

Buildings and Architecture: Agincourt to the Second World War

The Great Hall

Although its origins are obscure, we do know that the present Great Hall is not the first to be constructed on the Guildhall site. When the first one appeared we are not sure, possibly during the late Anglo-Saxon period. There is archaeological evidence that an earlier Great Hall existed by the late thirteenth century and the name of 'Guildhall Yard' was also commonly used from the late thirteenth century.

Nor is much is known about John Croxtone, the builder and designer of the present Great Hall, although we can assume that he was a master mason and had probably been involved in church building. The architecture of the Great Hall is cathedral-like and borrows much in style and execution from church construction of the time; it even faces west to east.

Croxtone was instructed to build a hall with no obstacles, pillars or aisles and large enough to house the Mayor's Court and Court of Aldermen. Although the interior of the Great Hall is nave-like, it departs from established church building by employing this open layout. When completed it was, and still is, the second largest single span great hall in Britain. Only Westminster Hall at the Houses of Parliament is larger.

Although we know little of Croxtone, we do know that he also worked under the master mason Henry Yevele during his rebuilding work at Westminster Hall. Originally built at the end of the eleventh century by King William II as part of the Palace of Westminster, Westminster Hall had recently been renovated by King Richard II. It's likely that Croxtone would have looked at the improvements, and the advances employed here, as inspiration for his new project.

Croxtone built his Hall in the English Perpendicular style, which dominated the later Gothic styles of the fifteenth and early sixteenth centuries. The Great Hall has eight bays on both north and south sides with large windows to east and west and was the largest building in the City of London apart from St Paul's Cathedral.

The Hall measured 151 x 48 feet and had an ornately painted, decorated interior. Discoveries in 1987 suggest that the dominant colours would have been green and

Above: The Great Hall from Guildhall Yard.

Below: Probable Guildhall Plan, fifteenth century.

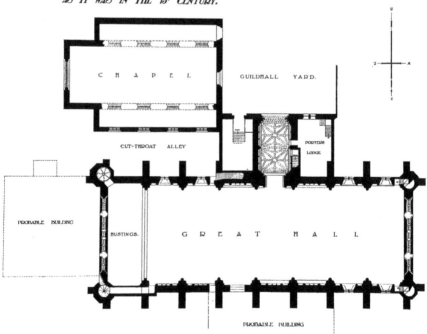

54

gold with a red lining-out. An ornate Gothic-style Porch served as entrance and antechamber to the Great Hall.

Croxtone's roof for the Great Hall has always been something of a mystery. It seems Croxtone prepared for stone arches but that budget constraints probably resulted in a pitched timber roof.

The exterior of the Great Hall was not smoothly finished or decorated to an exceptional level. There was no need. It's worth remembering that Guildhall was built in a crowded environment, narrow streets and alleys on all sides. Guildhall Yard was barely wider than the Porch. The full length of the Great Hall would have been obscured until you were actually standing within its vast interior. This narrow approach through the Yard, hemmed in by buildings to the east and west, was the layout that would have greeted the visitor until after the Second World War.

Funding for the Great Hall was raised by the Guilds as well as by bequests, fines, penalties and a 'scavage' tax on imported goods sold by foreigners. King Henry V also allowed 'free passage of lime, ragstone and freestone by land or water' for its construction. In 1423 the will of Richard Whittington helped to pay for the interior paving 'with hardstone of Purbeck' and for some of the windows. It's thought that the final completion was staggered until 1499, when two turrets were added.

On its completion the Guildhall consisted of the Great Hall, plus the Mayor's Court and Court of Aldermen (also known as the Inner Chamber) on the north side, with the Porch to the south and the crypts in the undercroft. To reflect its burgeoning use as a venue for banqueting and 'gaudy days', during the early sixteenth century a kitchen, buttery, pantry, ovens, larder and wine and ale cellars were added, all paid for by Sir John Shaw who had been knighted after the Battle of Bosworth in 1485. Banquets had previously been held at the Merchant Taylors' and Grocers' Halls.

A leathermarket was held in the undercroft of the buildings to the north, which were in use until the 1880s when they were demolished to make way for a new Court of Common Council. Perhaps the most notorious addition during the late fifteenth century, and kept especially for badly behaved apprentices, were 'two dismal prisons known as Little Ease' underneath the Hall Keeper's Office.

A boundary wall to Guildhall Yard's west side and a gatehouse on the southern boundary had existed, it's thought by the late thirteenth century. The entire Guildhall site was now surrounded by a wall, with a rebuilt gatehouse, to create a precinct around all of the buildings. This again borrowed from the construction of English cathedral buildings, which were all enclosed within a close.

Why was there this big push to build a complex of grand secular buildings during the early fifteenth century? Money may provide part of the answer. We can assume that the wealth now existed within the City to fund large parts of this 'status symbol' project. Influence may also have mattered, with wealthy merchants such as Richard Whittington able to develop, and bring support to, a Corporation project on such a grand scale.

Another reason may have been to emphasise the point that London was not just a trading city, but a mercantile centre capable of competing with the other great trading cities of continental Europe. Size mattered and the Great Hall was built on

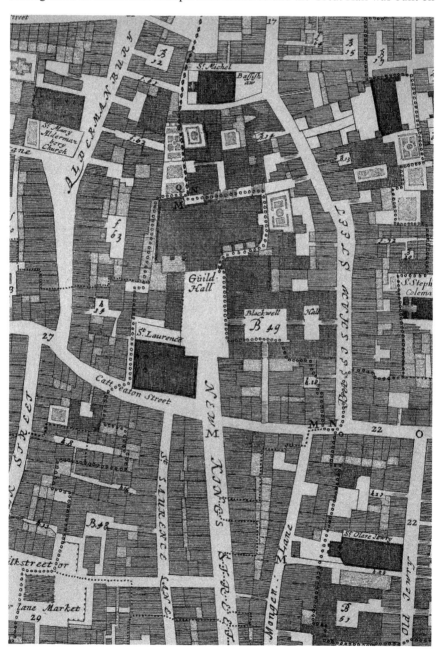

Detail of Ogilby and Morgan Map, 1667.

a scale to impress. At its centre presided its secular emperor, a man neither royal nor religious, but a trader: the Lord Mayor of the City of London.

Croxtone and his wife Anneys were given a house to live in on the north side of Guildhall. It's thought Croxtone died sometime between the years 1446 and 1451. His wages were 20 shillings per annum and this seems to have increased to 60 shillings, perhaps as a pension.

The areas of London affected by the Great Fire of 1666 went beyond Guildhall. Most of the Great Hall's roof was destroyed, but the interior of the Great Hall itself survived. Thomas Vincent, a puritan preacher who had witnessed and recorded the Great Fire wrote in *God's Terrible Voice in the City by Plague and Fire,* 'That night the sight of Guildhall was a fearful spectacle, which stood, the whole body of it together in view, for several hours together after the fire had taken it, without flames (I suppose because the timber was such solid oake) in a bright shining coale as if it had been a palace of gold.'

The new roof, intended as a temporary replacement, lasted for 200 years. This replacement was a flat timber roof, covered by a shallow layer of pitch. It was also higher than the old roof by between ten and twenty feet, with a clerestory (upper windows) adding more light. The new interior 'ceiling' was probably panelled in order to provide decoration and an illusion of depth.

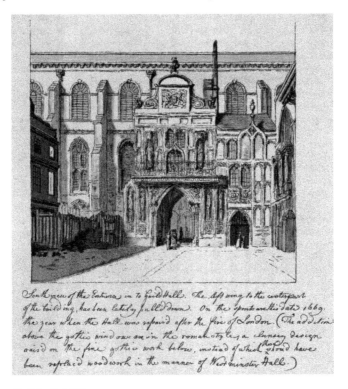

Guildhall, 1669.

Sir Christopher Wren.

Christopher Wren may have provided some oversight although his involvement is unclear and somewhat disputed. It seems likely that Peter Mills, the City Surveyor until 1671, oversaw and designed most aspects of the earlier repairs. It was not until 1671 that the interior repair of the Great Hall was completed and ready for use. A baroque-style gable was also added to the top of the Gothic porch at this time by, it would seem, either Mills or Wren.

The most significant legacy of Wren's involvement (with his colleague Robert Hooke) has nothing to do with Guildhall but is the street that leads from the River Thames north towards Guildhall. It seems such a natural approach today, but King Street and Queen Street did not exist at all until after the Great Fire. Ironmonger Lane and Lawrence Lane, two narrow streets that we would nowadays consider no wider than alleys, had been the main approaches since the early Middle Ages.

With the idea of greater visibility in mind, Wren also demolished the outer precinct wall and gates, or what little had survived the Great Fire. Instead of looking for inspiration towards the English cathedral, Wren was now looking more to Paris and Versailles, imitating the Continental fashion for openness and accessibility.

Full renovation and rebuilding would not occur until the 1860s when Sir Horace Jones, Surveyor to the City, began his extensive works. By the mid-nineteenth century, Gothic revivalism had become the fashionable architectural style of choice for many commissioners of public works, new churches and for many architects too.

Following its destruction by fire in 1834 the Houses of Parliament had been almost completely rebuilt in the Gothic style. Sir Charles Barry, assisted by Augustus Pugin, had by 1859 completed his new Parliament, which stands today as London's most distinctive example of this great British architectural fad.

Sir Horace Jones by contrast had an original and almost complete Gothic building with which to work. Where Gothic original had been replaced with Baroque or neoclassical renovation and repair, Jones re-Gothicised. Like John Croxtone four centuries earlier, Jones was inspired in part by the splendour of Westminster Hall.

The renovation process encompassed the clerestory windows, which disappeared, various other window tracery and masonry, the paved floor and most significantly the construction of a Westminster Hall-style hammer-beam roof, the like of which Croxtone hadn't previously constructed. Unfortunately for Jones it was always the opinion that his faux-medieval timber roof was a failure. It was regarded as heavy and squat, darkening what could have been a lighter space.

Above: The Great Hall, eighteenth century.

Below: Guildhall, 1755.

Guildhall Interior.

The Great Hall, late nineteenth century.

The north and south windows were restored with new stained glass designs depicting scenes from the City's history. A new screen to the east and a new gallery to the west were installed, both carved in Gothic style. New technology, in the form of gas pipes, were also fitted.

HORACE JONES, ARCHITECT.   W. GRIGGS, PHOTO-LITH.

Council Chamber, 1884.

The carving, guilding and painting were redone and reinterpreted to create a
Great Hall as it may have looked during its Plantagenet and Tudor heyday. The
memorials, where they were considered not Gothic enough, such as that to Nelson,
were stripped of overt Classical decoration where possible.

Horace Jones continued to redevelop the Guildhall site beyond the Great Hall.
His Council Chamber of 1884 was built to the north of the Great Hall, superseding a
not-so-old Council Chamber that had been built by George Dance the Younger in the
1780s. Jones's new Chamber was designed with twelve sides to resemble a cathedral
chapter house, picking up where Croxtone's original Gothic designs had left off.

THE LIBRARY AND MUSEUM OF THE CORPORATION OF THE CITY OF LONDON.

Above: Library and Museum, late nineteenth century.

Below: Horace Jones's Guildhall Plans.

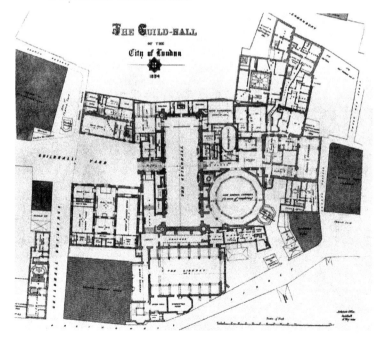

Of Jones's vast building works only the old museum and the old library remain intact. Both in keeping with the Gothic revivalist style employed by Jones elsewhere, they can today be viewed from the east side of the modern Guildhall complex from Basinghall Street. These buildings now house committee rooms and administration offices and are rented out for commercial hire and public functions. The old museum merged with the London Museum to form the Museum of London in 1975. The Council Chamber was destroyed by enemy action in the Second World War, its site now completely covered by the Guildhall North Wing, which was built post-war.

Sir Horace Jones (1819-87) was born within a five-minute walk of Guildhall in Bucklersbury. Apart from Sir Christopher Wren, Jones has arguably left the greatest architectural legacy extant in the City of London: Old Billingsgate Market, Leadenhall Market, Smithfield Market, Tower Bridge and Temple Bar Memorial.

Sir Horace Jones.

Guildhall Porch

The Porch at the time of John Croxtone resembled a large elaborate church porch, including niches for statues. A statue of Christ was at the apex, over the door. Statues representing Law and Learning were a level below on either side, and Prudence, Justice, Fortitude and Temperance were below them. There was also an entrance to the east crypt. These entrances were elaborately decorated as they faced onto Guildhall Yard and could easily be seen, whereas the rest of the walls were obscured by other buildings.

Approaching Guildhall from King Street now, the first building that can be seen looking north through Guildhall Yard is the porch to the Great Hall. This porch was designed by George Dance the Younger, Surveyor to the City almost a century before Sir Horace Jones. Dance's own architectural legacy at Guildhall has also enjoyed mixed fortunes.

As Surveyor to the City during the 1770s and 1780s, Dance was commissioned to design many adjustments to existing Guildhall buildings and offices. He was also put in charge of all the repairs that were necessary, the first since the Great Fire. These included works to the Great Hall, the various courts, and a new Council Chamber. Dance also designed a new terrace of offices to the west side of Guildhall Yard which survived until 1969.

The Great Hall and Porch today.

Among the many stone decorations on Croxtone's old porch were statues of Moses and Aaron representing Law and Learning and the Four Virtues: Prudence, Justice, Fortitude and Temperance. They are now on display at the Museum of London, but not before being sold off, lost and rediscovered in a Welsh garden in 1972.

Law and Learning and the Four Virtues.

BUILDINGS AND ARCHITECTURE

The Porch was designed to create a grand and imposing facade to Guildhall Yard, viewed from the south. Croxtone's Porch was intended to be a symbolic entrance to a building looking forward to a London sharing parity with Europe. Dance's Porch was to be a symbolic entrance to a building looking forward to global economic power.

The Porch is built as high as the Great Hall and was completed in 1789. It replaced the old porch that Dance had been commissioned to demolish. His building is a contradictory mix of bold and playful and a significant blend of old and new. The style, relatively unique, is described as 'Hindoo Gothic', although it integrates elements of Croxtone's Gothic with the neoclassical fashions of Dance's time.

The question concerning the Porch has tended to be, why 'Hindoo Gothic'? Dance was an experimental and creative designer at the same time that the inclusion of India into the Empire was progressing apace. Eastern influences were beginning to be felt, including within the arts. Dance's friend, the artist William Hodges, had recently returned from India and some of his paintings of Indian landscapes, exhibited at the Royal Academy in 1786, would surely have been seen by Dance.

Sir Joshua Reynolds, President of the Royal Academy, said of Hodges' exhibition, 'The barbaric splendour of those Asiatic buildings, which are now publishing by a member of this Academy may possibly... furnish an architect... with hints of composition and general effect that would not otherwise have occurred.'

The Indian details, which can be seen most visibly in the windows and the outline of the turrets, are clearly a nod to the eastern influences newly imported from the far reaches of Empire. It's entirely possible to interpret Dance's porch as a statement of the new reality too: a patriotic gesture and affirmation of Britain's expanding Imperial interests.

The interior of John Croxtone's original porch can still be seen when entering the Great Hall through the Porch from Guildhall Yard. His low, vaulted ceiling, again borrowing from church architecture, is enveloped by Dance's radical new building. The old demolished porch would have been decorated and impressive, even then an appropriate entrance to the grandeur of the Great Hall.

George Dance the Younger.

The Coat of Arms of the City of London was first displayed in 1381, with two lions supporting. It was not until 1609 that two dragons appeared on the seal and that the motto was used. At the top of the central tower of the Porch sits one version of the old coat of arms. At its centre is the Shield of St George. In the top left quarter of the shield is the sword of St Paul, patron saint of the City. To the left and right of the shield are two supporting dragons. The shield is surmounted by the Muscovy Hat worn by the Swordbearer to the Lord Mayor, which symbolises the City's ancient connections to trade. Two maces are sculpted in relief onto the fluted pilasters on either side of the coat of arms. The mace, carried during ceremonies by the Serjeant-at-Arms, represents the authority of the Lord Mayor. Underneath the coat of arms is the motto of the City of London: *Domine Dirige Nos*, or Lord, Guide Us.

The coat of arms displayed on the Alderman's Court to the west side of the Yard is the modern version. The present version was only obtained from the College of Arms in 1957. At its top is displayed a silver and red wreath with the left wing of a dragon in silver and a red cross on its underside. Red crosses can also be seen on the undersides of the two supporting dragons' wings.

City coat of arms on the Porch.

The Crypts

Beneath the Great Hall lies the undercroft, split into two ancient crypts. The East Crypt and West Crypt together correspond to the footprint of the Great Hall above them. It was believed for many years that the East Crypt was older but we know now that the West Crypt is the older of the two.

As far back as anyone could remember, the West Crypt had just been used for storing records and other materials. Following its restoration in 1973 we now know why it was thought to be newer. Much of the West Crypt had been barrel-vaulted with bricks since being damaged during the Great Fire of 1666. Until the brickwork had been removed, exposing the original stone work, it wasn't possible to assess the crypt properly. It's now thought the West Crypt dates to the late thirteenth or early fourteenth centuries and this makes it significantly older than the Great Hall.

The stonework of the West Crypt is quite plain, stands eleven feet high and is five bays long. The octagonal piers are undecorated, have no capitals and rise directly into the vaults. There is speculation that it may once have been 'L' shaped and may even have been the floor of an earlier Guildhall, referred to in Chapter 1. The new stonework reflects the old. The paving is York stone with Doulton and Portland stone being used in the repair of the columns.

The East Crypt by comparison is well studied, although some mystery still remains. Built by John Croxtone, it is slightly higher at thirteen feet and too finely decorated to

West Crypt.

be used solely for storage. It is four bays long and like the West Crypt has clustered pillars. These pillars have shiny Purbeck marble shafts, Mansfield stone capitals and Godstone sandstone bases. The vaulted ceilings' carved bosses, with groins, display various painted coats of arms, including those of King Edward the Confessor.

East Crypt.

Stained glass windows in the Crypt, by Brian Thomas.

The East Crypt is clearly designed with more care and expense and again there is some speculation as to why. Could it have been intended for banquets or entertainment? The East Crypt was restored in 1961 with new stained-glass windows by Brian Thomas, who ten years later made the windows for the restored West Crypt.

The Library

There have been three libraries at Guildhall and it makes a claim to being the earliest public library to be maintained by a local authority. The original library was established during the building of Croxtone's Great Hall in 1425, at the behest of John Carpenter, Common Clerk to the City of London. Carpenter was an executor to the will of former Lord Mayor Richard Whittington who had bequeathed some of the funds to make the building possible. Carpenter's own will in 1444 made possible the foundation of the City of London School.

A small library had already been established within the Guildhall chapel and college and Croxtone's new building works provided the opportunity to create a new, larger library. As is often the case with smaller projects that fall within the orbit of a bigger development, funding was an issue and the library was not completed until the 1450s. It was a decent sized building, established to the south of Guildhall chapel, measuring approximately 90 x 56 feet, and was described as modest and well lit. There were three chambers on the ground level and one large upper room with twenty-eight desks.

Chained Bible. Permission Guildhall Library.

The library was run by the Dominicans, also known as the Blackfriars or Preaching Friars, and the books were exclusively theological, or 'for education in Divine Scriptures'. The building was constructed of stone, had a slate roof, and consisted of three chambers on the ground floor and one upper storey for the books, which were chained to the desks and bookshelves. Some of the earliest library keepers were buried within the neighbouring chapel, priests such as John Clipstone and Thomas Mason.

With the Reformation came instability and the library's end. In 1549, during the reign of King Edward VI, the Lord Protector

Duke of Somerset essentially stole the library. While building his new palace at Somerset House, near the Strand, he sent over some carts to remove the books so that he could borrow them. The books were never returned and the library ceased to exist.

It was generally said that 'covetousness was at that time so busy about private commodity that public wealth was not anymore regarded'. It is also possible that as a quid pro quo for the library books the Corporation was allowed to buy back the dissolved chapel building in 1550, for which it had been petitioning Somerset and the King. The wheels turned slowly but eventually in 1824 a committee was established to inquire 'into the best mode of arranging and carrying into effect in the Guildhall a library of all matters relating to the City, the Borough of Southwark and the County of Middlesex'.

In 1828 a new library was established containing over 1,380 works. Expansion was fast and its reputation grew. By the 1860s a new library building was central to the new plans and in 1873 Horace Jones's Gothic revivalist library officially opened, having been built on the site of what was described as 'some old and dilapidated houses on Basinghall Street'. It still stands today, better known as the Old Library, and is mainly used for events and functions – as is the old Museum, which occupies the lower floor, level with the crypts.

Guildhall Library logo,
late nineteenth century.

Devoted as it was to books, Jones created a devotional church-like library to house the collection. Standing at 100 feet x 65 x 50, it features a nave and aisles, twenty-eight clerestory windows, and great perpendicular stained-glass windows to the north and south. The roof is supported by twelve arched ribs, each one featuring the coat of arms of the Great Twelve Guilds. Surprisingly, for a space so full of paper, the Old Library has three fireplaces – although they are no longer used. The flume on the north side runs through the hollow tracery of the great north window above the fireplace, which is how the smoke was, in the past, harmlessly expelled.

True to its brief of 1824, the library specialized in the history, topography and antiquities of London and included books, prints, drawings and pamphlets. By 1938 it held 126,000 books and 21,000 manuscripts. The air raid that destroyed much of the Great Hall on 29 December 1940, and another in May 1941, also caused damage to the library. Although many works had been relocated, over 25,000 volumes were lost. Through perseverance and the war spirit the library reopened in October 1942.

Guildhall Library, late nineteenth century engraving.

The Old Library today.

Public art decorates this former public space. Carved by J.W. Seale, the spandrel of each arch within the old library features busts of the famous, representing history, poetry, printing, architecture, sculpture, painting, philosophy, law, medicine, music, astronomy, geography, natural history and botany. Sculpted for each theme are Stow, Camden, Shakespeare, Milton, Gutenberg, Caxton, William of Wykeham, Wren, Michelangelo, Flaxman, Holbein, Hogarth, Bacon, Locke, Coke, Blackstone, Harvey, Sydenham, Purcell, Handel, Galileo, Newton, Columbus, Raleigh, Linnaeus, Cuvier, Ray and Gerard. In the context of Imperial Britain, this placed great Britons squarely within the firmament of the universal greats

The Old Library spandrels (Shakespeare is on the right).

Chapter 6

Buildings and Architecture: Second World War Onwards

During the 1930s the Corporation asked the architect Giles Gilbert Scott to provide advice for the redevelopment of Guildhall Yard. Gilbert Scott proposed comprehensive plans that involved changing the shape of Guildhall Yard from rectangular to circular and building a new museum and art gallery, both to the east side. A new court house and offices would also be built to the south and the north.

Preliminary permissions were granted in December 1938, but the Second World War imposed a hiatus on all thoughts of progress. On 29 December 1940 Guildhall was bombed in an air raid and extensively damaged. Many buildings were damaged beyond repair. The site would not be revisited by Gilbert Scott until 1948.

Guildhall Yard between the world wars.

The Great Hall, blitzed, 29 December 1940.

On his return to Guildhall after the war Gilbert Scott was faced with a project to rebuild, not repair. Sir Horace Jones's Council Chamber and all of the offices to the north of the Great Hall had been razed to the ground. The Great Hall had been left open to the elements following the bombing, its roof completely destroyed in the fire storm. A temporary roof covering provided an interim stop-gap.

Internally a complete renovation of the Great Hall was required and the repair of many of the memorials. The head of Neptune on the memorial to Horatio Nelson had been blown off and the timber statues of Gog and Magog, London's mythical guardians, were guarding no more. They had been burned to a cinder.

The Art Gallery to the east side of Guildhall Yard was all but destroyed and a completely new building would be required to house the Guildhall art collection. Whereas before the war new office buildings were proposed, they were now a necessity.

Work began in November 1953.

The Great Hall

Restoration of the Great Hall was completed on 30 October 1954, just in time for the Lord Mayor's Banquet on 9 November. Instantly noticeable were the stone arches which raised and supported the new English oak roof. Should fire ever destroy the Great Hall again, puritan preacher Thomas Vincent would surely recognise and again mourn this stone and timber 'pallace of gold'.

New clerestory windows provided the extra light that was needed, cleverly introduced within the pre-existing pitch of the roof. The gable walls at the east and west ends had withstood the bombing, meaning Gilbert Scott's roof had to conform to previous dimensions.

The Great Hall today.

What had not survived of the windows was the stained glass. Gilbert Scott designed a new and utilitarian pattern that could be repeated in each window, on all sides. What we see today is a patterned chevron design bearing the names of all the Lord Mayors since Henry Fitzailwyn and the names all the Monarchs under whom they served. This 'modern' tradition continues today when the name of each new Lord Mayor is added to a list of their predecessors.

Gilbert Scott needed to replace most of the woodwork too. The panelling and new galleries were carved out of English oak in the Gothic style. Some oak panelling did survive the war and this was subsequently treated with a bleaching agent. Large bronze chandeliers were hung on the north and south sides.

The Portland stone floor, with black tiles inlaid in bands and around the border, was re-laid with under-floor heating. The paving is now covered in wall-to-wall red carpet tiles, which seems to dull the impact in one of London's great indoor spaces. The Great Hall is in use so often it was decided that carpet was needed to protect the paving. It's partially lifted, very rarely, for some ceremonials in the shape of a 'T', 'L' or three tiles wide.

Banners of the Great Twelve Guilds hang from the clerestory level and the shields of the other Livery Companies are displayed above, almost at cornice level. The sculptured memorials and monuments were repaired where necessary and in the case of Gog and Magog replaced completely.

Externally the spire is constructed on a lead skeleton and where wood is used, for instance at the base and lantern, it is teak.

Giles Gilbert Scott's Great Hall, like Horace Jones's Great Hall, is a mix of respect for tradition and functionality. Both architects were amongst their century's greatest designers of buildings and both architects gave themselves permission to create a Guildhall that mirrored something that they thought was authentic. Gilbert Scott's renovation seems to be universally admired in a way that Jones's never was.

The specification of the oak required by Gilbert Scott meant that the wood had to come from trees that had been felled for at least four years and then aired for three months. The 134 oak trees felled had to be over 150 years old and were sourced in Kent and Scotland.

The North Wing

To the north of the Great Hall, the Council Chamber and offices had also been destroyed by enemy action. Giles Gilbert Scott proposed a brick office building and this was completed in 1957.

Gilbert Scott had been a consultant architect for Battersea Power Station pre-war and was working on the design and build of Bankside Power Station during these early post-war years too (now the Tate Modern). The style of both power stations is

Guildhall North Wing.

sometimes referred to as 'brick-cathedral'. Gilbert Scott was also architect of the well-recognised, brick-dominated Anglican Liverpool Cathedral.

Guildhall North Wing certainly borrows from this 'brick-cathedral' style, similarly employing dark brick and being symmetrical in design. It is regarded as being somewhat austere, the only decoration in the brickwork being some Dutch-style brick motifs above the upper storey windows. The ground levels along the North Wing have geometric, modernist stone decoration. To either side of the east and west entrances are stone columns surmounted by City dragons.

The West Wing

Sir Giles Gilbert Scott died in 1960 but had already passed on the management of the Guildhall project to his son Richard. The younger Gilbert Scott led the way for a contemporary Guildhall Yard and proposed five new construction projects which externally dominate the Guildhall we see today: an enlarged Guildhall Yard, a new West Wing encompassing offices, a new library, a new art gallery on the east side, an ambulatory linking the Great Hall to the West Wing, and restoration of the crypts.

Gilbert Scott took a practical view of the project, given the time it would take to complete and that the project would progress in stages. The West Wing would not necessarily conform to the symmetry his father had endowed to the rather plain North Wing. There would be a loose informality and Gilbert Scott would introduce new architectural ideas.

These new ideas included the 'New Brutalism', a heavy geometric style, often employing concrete and brick. Gilbert Scott also wanted to introduce some playfulness to his buildings and there were two high profile projects which may have inspired his final designs. The first project was close to Guildhall. Finnish born American architect Eero Saarinen was completing the new US Embassy at Grosvenor Square in Mayfair. It was spiky, it was glossy, and it made a feature of its geometric concrete finish.

Much further away was the vast Oscar Niemeyer project to build Brasilia, a new capital city for Brazil. Imaginatively executed and dominated by concrete structures, there was a light and rhythmic movement to the new public buildings that was appealing to architects all over the world. It epitomised the modern thinking in architecture and it was revolutionary. Gilbert Scott, however, did not completely dispense with Gothic, as can be seen in the pointed windows and arches of the West Wing and the cloistered 'vaulted' feel of the Ambulatory.

The brief that Gilbert Scott had to satisfy was quite complex. The West Wing was to have a number of functions which included offices, committee rooms, a Court of Aldermen, the new library, an underground car park and on the top storeys small flats for overnight accommodation by councillors.

One of the most significant features of the development was the opening up of Guildhall Yard. This created mixed emotions, as the Yard up until then had been narrow and enclosed and not much wider than the Porch. Gilbert Scott proposed that it should now be wide open and public, no longer intimate or claustrophobic. In the process Gilbert Scott also demolished George Dance the Younger's terraced offices of the 1790s. In exposing the Great Hall, and by creating a more publicly

Guildhall West Wing, Court of Aldermen and Ambulatory.

Guildhall Yard.

accessible Guildhall, Gilbert Scott was carrying on what Christopher Wren started after the Great Fire.

The West Wing is L-shaped, extending around to the north. The most noticeable part of the building perhaps is the Court of Aldermen. This brutal polygonal structure juts out into the Yard and is only accessible by a bridge link from inside the West Wing. It is constructed, like the rest of the West Wing, out of precast concrete panels and is supported on four precast concrete columns. The coat of arms of the City of London is displayed on its east wall.

On its completion in 1974 the West Wing was well received, nominated for awards, and although 'tradition is maintained' was also described as 'discreetly modern'.

Guildhall Art Gallery

Following the almost total destruction of the Art Gallery during the Second World War, a temporary gallery was constructed in 1946 within the bombed-out remains of the old building in Guildhall Yard. Steel girders supported the roof, which was made of straw and asphalt blocks, and the floor was laid with lino. It utilised, as best as it could, part of the surviving façade, but was described gloomily as 'barn like'.

The new art gallery had been intended for completion by 1976, but instead funds were channelled towards the building of the West Wing and new library. By 1985 it was decided that the 'old eyesore' and the vacant, debris-strewn ground behind the Gallery had to go. Richard Gilbert Scott was appointed to design the new gallery.

79

Guildhall Art Gallery.

Gilbert Scott's West Wing had been well received and he and the Corporation were well acquainted. Still, Gilbert Scott's first design was turned down and the building we see today is his second proposal.

The temporary gallery was demolished in 1987. It was still abutting the south-east side of the Great Hall and the Porch. Gilbert Scott would now have the opportunity to open up the entire east side of Guildhall Yard to mirror the exposed Yard to the west.

Prior to construction, the Museum of London Archaeological Service (MoLAS) came on site to carry out an inspection of the cleared ground. They set to work and found Saxon remains, which didn't surprise them. Then they made what could be called the archaeological discovery of the late twentieth century, the Roman amphitheatre.

The site was immediately designated an ancient monument. There would subsequently be a decade-long delay and a redesign was called for, which required enclosing the remains of the amphitheatre within the new gallery building. Gilbert Scott eventually appeared quite relaxed saying, 'The idea is that it becomes part of the Art Gallery. It was an extraordinary bit of luck. The Amphitheatre takes the shape of Guildhall Yard'.

The Art Gallery was opened in 1999 and, like his West Wing, was hailed as a successful building project, although its design is nothing like his earlier West Wing concept. Not totally Brutalist, slightly more post-Modernist, it blends architectural styles and could be described as 'Gothic Brutalism'.

The façade is in sympathy with the style of both the Great Hall and the Porch, its six bay windows and window tracery resembling a kind of stripped-down Gothic. The building is faced in Portland stone, and Cotswold slates line the pitched roof. The Art Gallery itself takes up three floors; the Amphitheatre is suspended at basement level. Remarkably two more levels are submerged below.

When standing in the centre of Guildhall Yard one can observe an elliptical shape in dark grey paving which traces the outline of the Amphitheatre. As Gilbert Scott observed, it does take the shape of the Yard. Starting from the Art Gallery around to the Church of St Lawrence Jewry, past the Court of Aldermen, curving in front of the Porch and returning to the Art Gallery, the shape and size of Roman London's main entertainment venue is now clearly visible in twenty-first century London.

Who were the Gilbert Scotts? There have been quite a few architectural dynasties working in London, ever since Christopher Wren Junior followed in his father's footsteps. The Gilbert Scotts surely rank as the greatest of them all.

Sir George Gilbert Scott (1811-78). Son of a clergyman from Buckinghamshire and founder of the dynasty. Along with Augustus Pugin (himself part of an architectural dynasty) he became the greatest exponent of Gothic Revivalism during the nineteenth century. Approximately 166 building projects were built or restored by Gilbert Scott Senior. His most well-known projects in London include: Midland Grand Hotel, St Pancras Station (1874), The Foreign & Commonwealth Office, Whitehall (1868) and the Albert Memorial, Kensington Gardens (1872).

Sir George Gilbert Scott.

George Gilbert Scott Junior (1839-97). He worked with his father but not many buildings have his name on them. Many of his solo London projects have been demolished or were bombed in the Second World War. He died in the Midland Grand Hotel.

Sir Giles Gilbert Scott (1880-1960). Son of George Junior and like his grandfather Sir George, Sir Giles was an incredibly prolific architect. He was loyal to his Gothic revivalist roots but also ventured successfully into modernism. As well as designing Liverpool Cathedral (1903-60) his best known London projects

Sir Giles Gilbert Scott.

Richard Gilbert Scott.

include: Battersea Power Station (1929-35), Waterloo Bridge (1940), Bankside Power Station (now the Tate Modern, 1960) and his work at Guildhall (1953-58). Possibly his most famous design is not a building, it's the red telephone box, which he originally wanted to be silver with a green interior (K2 - 1924, K3 - 1930, K6 - 1935).

Richard Gilbert Scott (1923-2017). Preferring to be known as Dick Scott, he has designed three churches which have achieved Grade II listing already. He worked with Sir Giles on the Guildhall projects and took over when his father retired. Dick Scott bridged styles and fashions throughout his career, from modernist to brutalist to post-modern. All these styles can be seen in his work at Guildhall, in projects which dominated the rest of his career (1960-99).

John Oldrid Scott (1841-1913) who was the brother of George Junior. Over thirty-five church buildings or restorations have his name but most famous is his design for St Sophia's Greek Orthodox Cathedral in Bayswater, London W2.

Adrian Gilbert Scott (1882-1963) was the younger brother of Sir Giles and similarly straddled both Gothic and modernist design. The church of St Mary & St Joseph on the Lansbury Estate, Poplar, is one of his designs and he restored St Albans, Holborn, after the Second World War.

Elisabeth Scott (1898-1972) was the great-niece of George Gilbert Scott and one of the first students to study at the Architectural Association in Bedford Square, London WC1. Scott won the competition to design the Shakespeare Memorial Theatre, Stratford-upon-Avon (1932, now replaced by the Royal Shakespeare Theatre). This was the first public building to be designed by a female architect.

Chapter 7

The Lord Mayor of the City of London

Guildhall, as well as being a historical building, is the City of London town hall, where the City of London Corporation is based, presided over by the Lord Mayor. The Lord Mayor is also head of the Court of Aldermen and the Court of Common Council, its governing bodies.

It is important not to confuse the Lord Mayor of London with the Mayor of London. The Lord Mayor is Mayor of the City of London, also known as the Square Mile. The Mayor is the elected Mayor of Greater London, incorporating all the London boroughs. Lord Mayor of London is one of the world's oldest continuously held civic offices.

The Lord Mayor is not only Lord Mayor of the City of London. His titles include the Admiral of the Port of London, Rector of City University, Vice-President of Birkbeck College, Chief Magistrate of the City of London, Member of the Accession Council, Governor of the Honourable Artillery Company, Clerk of the City Markets, President of Gresham College, President of the City of London Reserve Forces and Cadets Association, Trustee of St Paul's Cathedral, Patron of the City Livery Club, Patron of the United Wards Club, Patron of the Guild of Freemen of the City of London, and he also heads the City's Commission of Lieutenancy, representing the Sovereign in the City of London.

Robert Titchborn, Lord Mayor 1657.

83

Royal Luncheon at the Guildhall, 10th March 1961. Tony Cuneo. Permission of Guildhall Art Gallery. Queen Elizabeth II and the Lord Mayor seated at the top table on the Dais.

He or she is also known as the Right Honourable the Lord Mayor. Within the City of London only the Sovereign outranks the Lord Mayor. Sources vary but it is believed the Mayor became known as Lord Mayor in 1354 under King Edward III when the incumbent Mayor was Thomas Legge.

Lord Mayors are apolitical and have many social and ceremonial duties. A very important job is to promote the City of London and they will spend a significant part of their year in office abroad representing the City and its interests. He or she has cabinet minister status when doing this.

The Lord Mayor's traditional formal dress consists of white shirt with lace cuffs and jabot stock, which is a kind of wide cravat, and a black velvet court dress coat with waistcoat and knee breeches. The Mayor also wears black silk stockings and patent court shoes with steel buckles. The Lord Mayor's hat is a black beaver plush tricorn hat with black ostrich feathers. There are many other articles of formal dress, including robes, which the Lord Mayor wears on different official occasions.

The mayoral insignia consists of the chain of office – a 'collar of esses', twenty-eight 'S' shaped links, alternating roses and knots made of gold and enamel – and the Mayoral Jewel, which hangs from a link shaped like a Tudor portcullis. The collar was donated to the office by Sir John Aleyn, Lord Mayor in 1525 and 1535, in his will of 1545.

The original Jewel or badge that is attached to the collar was presented to the City by Sir Martin Bowes, Lord Mayor in 1558. In 1607 the Court of Aldermen acquired a new one which was replaced again by Rundell, Bridge and Company in 1803. The centre of this badge remains in the current Jewel, featuring the City arms and motto. The present encircling wreath of diamond set roses, shamrocks and thistles replaced an earlier one in 1866. In 1969 the setting for the diamonds was replaced.

A sword and mace are carried before the Lord Mayor on ceremonial occasions.

The City has five Swords. The Sword of State, dated to about 1680 and a symbol of the Lord Mayor's authority, is carried before the Lord Mayor. The pommel features figures of Justice and Fame and the sheath is red velvet. The Pearl Sword is sixteenth century with a scabbard decorated with pearls and is carried by the Lord Mayor on great occasions. The Old Bailey Sword probably dates from the sixteenth century, with a decorated purple velvet sheath. In the Central Criminal Court it is placed above the Lord Mayor's chair on the first and second days of each session and then in the Court of the Senior Commissioner.

The Black or Mourning Sword is used for occasions of solemnity and mourning. In 1534 there is mention of a sword with a black sheath but although the present one is not particularly old it does have an old blade. The Mansion House Justice Room Sword dates from the nineteenth century and is placed above the magistrate's chair in the Justice Room. It can be found at the Magistrate's Court at 1 Queen Victoria Street, EC4.

The Mace is five feet three inches long and made of silver gilt. It was made in 1735 by John White of London. Previous maces were made in 1559, 1627, 1649

The Lord Mayor's official limousine.

and 1660. It is surmounted by a royal crown, orb and cross. Under these are the royal arms and a cipher of King George III. The head is divided into four parts, one featuring a rose and thistle, one a fleur-de-lis, and one a harp, all with a crown and King George II's cipher. The fourth features the City arms. The shaft has decorated knobs (or knops) with inscriptions, including some referring to the Lord Mayor and Common Cryer and Sergeant at Arms of 1735.

The Crystal Mace or 'sceptre' probably dates from the fifteenth century. The shaft and knops are made out of crystal. The head is a gold coronet of fleur-de-lis and crosses with pearls, uncut sapphires and rubies. There is a royal coat of arms on the flat top. It is only seen when a new Lord Mayor is admitted to office when it is passed from the old Lord Mayor to the new, and at coronations, when the Lord Mayor carries it.

The City Purse is a red cloth bag embroidered with leaf work, gold scrolls and the City arms. It may be Elizabethan or early seventeenth century. It contains the Mayoralty Seal when one Lord Mayor passes the Seal on to the next.

The Seal first appeared in the late thirteenth century. From 1292 it was attached to documents in the name of the Mayor and Aldermen and from 1813-14 to documents issued by the Lord Mayor alone. The original seal featured St Thomas à Becket and St Paul. This was destroyed in 1381 and a new one was commissioned by William Walworth while he was Mayor, which kept Becket and St Paul and added other features including the Virgin and Child and the City arms. In 1912 it was replaced again and kept more or less the same but with two Tudor roses added.

To become Lord Mayor a person must be a Freeman of the City of London, an Alderman, and have previously served as one of the two Sheriffs of the City of London. They are voted for annually on Michaelmas Day, 29 September, or on the closest weekday, by liverymen (usually by acclamation, exceptionally by ballot) and then Aldermen (by ballot) at a meeting known as Common Hall. At the time of writing there have been two women Lord Mayors – they are not known as Mayoresses (a mayoress is the wife of a mayor). The first was Dame Mary Donaldson (1983) and the second was Dame Fiona Woolf (2013).

On the Friday preceding the second Saturday in November the Lord Mayor is sworn in at a ceremony known as the Silent Ceremony in Guildhall, where the symbols of office are passed to the new Lord Mayor from the previous Lord Mayor. It is conducted in silence, apart from the new Lord Mayor's declaration. After that, on the Saturday, comes the Lord Mayor's Show, which everyone can watch processing through the streets of the City.

On the following Monday the new Lord Mayor holds a banquet for the old Lord Mayor. This takes place in Guildhall, with the Lord Mayor's symbols of office, the sword and the mace on display. Guests include the Prime Minister, representatives of the Commonwealth and other countries and leaders of the armed services, the church and the judiciary.

The Lord Mayor's Show began in 1215 under King John, during which the Mayor had to swear allegiance to the King and be 'shown' to the people – hence

LORD MAYOR'S BANQUET *at the* GUILDHALL

H.R.H. Prince Arthur of Connaught, His Grace the Archbishop of Canterbury, the Prime Minister, and the Lord Chief Justice of England are seen at the high table.

Right: Lord Mayor's Banquet, 1914.

Below: *The Ninth of November 1888*. William Logsdail, 1890. Permission of Guildhall Art Gallery.

Lord Mayor's 'show'. Until 1856 the celebrations usually included a procession on the river involving a flotilla of the Livery Companies' ornate barges. This is probably where the expression carnival 'floats' comes from.

The Lord Mayor's coach, built in 1757, is on view at Guildhall a week or two before the actual procession. It starts at the Mansion House, pauses at St Paul's Cathedral for a blessing, stops at the Royal Courts of Justice where the Mayor swears allegiance to the sovereign, and returns to Mansion House again. In the evening there is a grand firework display on the River Thames.

Mansion House has been the official residence of the Lord Mayor since its completion by George Dance the Elder in 1752. Guildhall is the Lord Mayor's town hall, where the council meets. Mansion House is opposite the Royal Exchange and the Bank of England on the south side of Bank Junction.

Mansion House is a venue for entertaining visiting dignitaries, cabinet ministers and other public figures, as well as hosting an annual dinner at which the Chancellor of the Exchequer makes a speech on the state of the British economy.

Lord Mayors of Interest

Henry Fitzailwyn

London's first Mayor was Henry Fitzailwyn de Londonstone in 1189. Before that London was governed by a portreeve, appointed by the king. Fitzailwyn served every year until his death in 1212 and was the only mayor to hold the

post for life. He was a wealthy merchant who probably dealt in cloth. London was badly affected by fires at this time and Fitzailwyn was known for trying to encourage people to make buildings out of stone. Another of his actions was to raise money in London to ransom King Richard I who had been captured on his way back from the crusades.

The post of Mayor was created because King Richard I was becoming increasingly dependent on loans from the City for his wars and the City needed representation. The Mayor was initially appointed by the sovereign. In 1215 King John awarded London a charter, allowing the yearly election of a mayor by the citizens, so long as the mayor swore an oath of allegiance to the sovereign.

Henry Fitzailwyn.

> * (12) No 'scutage' or 'aid' may be levied in our kingdom without its general consent, unless it is for the ransom of our person, to make our eldest son a knight, and (once) to marry our eldest daughter. For these purposes only a reasonable 'aid' may be levied. 'Aids' from the city of London are to be treated similarly.
>
> + (13) **The city of London shall enjoy all its ancient liberties and free customs, both by land and by water.** We also will and grant that all other cities, boroughs, towns, and ports shall enjoy all their liberties and free customs.
>
> * (14) To obtain the general consent of the realm for the assessment of an 'aid' - except in the three cases specified above - or a 'scutage', we will cause the archbishops, bishops, abbots, earls, and greater barons to be summoned individually by letter. To those who hold lands directly of us we will cause a

Magna Carta

William Hardel

William Hardel was Sheriff in 1207 and Mayor in 1215. In 1215 King John famously sealed Magna Carta, a charter of political rights and liberties. William Hardel was one of the twenty-five people appointed to make sure the king kept to Magna Carta's terms, including that 'the city of London shall enjoy all its ancient liberties and free customs, both by land and by water.'

Sir William Walworth

Sir William Walworth was twice Lord Mayor, in 1374-5 and 1380-81 and was also Member of Parliament for the City. He was a member of the Fishmonger's Guild and was involved in arranging loans from the City to King Richard II.

He's also famous for having killed Wat Tyler, the leader of the Peasants' Revolt. In 1381 Wat Tyler and his followers advanced on London from Kent, along with another group advancing from Essex, protesting against serfdom and the Poll Tax. Tyler and his men entered London from the south, crossing London

Sir William Walworth.

Bridge. They opened prisons, destroyed law books and killed anyone they found who was connected with the government. When Wat Tyler met King Richard II to parley at Smithfield, just outside the City, Walworth killed him with a dagger for allegedly being disrespectful to the King.

Walworth raised the City's forces to defend the King against the insurgents and was awarded a knighthood and a pension in return. The dagger that he is said to have used to kill Wat Tyler is on display in Fishmongers' Hall, the Livery Hall of the Fishmongers Guild. There is also a stained-glass window of the scene in the Mansion House and a statue of him on Holborn Viaduct.

Richard Whittington

Surely the most famous Lord Mayor of London is Dick Whittington, who was a real person. His life story has been transformed into a storybook legend, which we often see depicted in pantomime. Here is the fictional story.

Dick was a poor boy from the country who decided to seek his fortune in London where he believed the streets were paved with gold. Walking to the city with his cat he managed to get a job as a kitchen scullion with Alderman Fitzwarren, a wealthy man.

Dick found the life hard. He had to sleep in the kitchen with the rats, and the housekeeper, who didn't like him, would often beat him. At least his cat managed to catch the rats and keep them away and his master's daughter Alice was nice to him as well. One day Alderman Fitzwarren sent one of his ships called the *Unicorn* on a trading expedition to the Barbary Coast. It was his custom to get everyone in the house to send something on the ship to trade. All Dick had was his cat, so he sent that. When the ship reached the Barbary Coast the prince there was suffering from an infestation of rats and mice, but no cat to catch them. Dick's cat did a wonderful job in getting rid of the rats and in gratitude the prince gave the traders a large pot of gold to take back to the cat's owner.

Meanwhile Dick had despaired of making his fortune and he decided to return home. As he walked up Highgate Hill on the outskirts of London he heard St Mary le Bow church bells ringing and they seemed to him to be saying, 'Turn again Whittington, three times Lord Mayor of London'. So he decided to try his luck again and turned back down the hill (there is a statue of a cat half way up the hill to commemorate this. The church of St Mary le Bow is still standing, though much altered by Sir Christopher Wren after the Great Fire of London).

Soon the *Unicorn* returned, Dick's money was given to him and he became very rich. He was able to go into partnership with Alderman Fitzwarren and marry his daughter Alice. Soon he too became an Alderman and eventually Lord Mayor three times.

Whittington's real life story is very different.

Richard Whittington was born in Pauntley in the Forest of Dean, Gloucestershire, in the 1350s. His father was Sir William Whittington, a wealthy landowner. But as Richard was not the eldest son he would not be entitled to inherit. He went to London instead to train as a mercer. Mercers dealt in high quality cloth such as silks, velvets and linen and other luxury goods and were also involved in the wool trade. He did well and became a member of the Mercer's Guild. A lot of his customers were wealthy, including the nobility and royalty, and he had dealings with King Richard II himself. By 1388 he had moved into money-lending, again the King being one of his clients. Whittington made around sixty loans to the crown.

In 1384 he became a Common Councillor and by 1393 he was an Alderman and became Sheriff. In June 1397 the incumbent Lord Mayor died and King Richard II appointed Whittington as his replacement. His first conventional term began in October 1397 – this accounts for the controversy over whether he was three or four times Lord Mayor of London. When King Henry IV supplanted King Richard II it did not affect Whittington as they had already had dealings and he was soon making loans to the new king.

He became Lord Mayor again in 1406 and 1419. So, four times Lord Mayor of London. In 1416 he became a Member of Parliament.

Whittington also loaned money to King Henry V. He married Alice Fitzwarin – this part of the pantomime is almost correct – and they had no children. He bought a house in 1402 next to the church of St Michael Paternoster Royal and in 1409 he started rebuilding the church. He died in 1423 and was originally buried in the church. Although he was looked on favourably by kings and nobility he was not knighted – so he is not referred to as Sir Richard Whittington.

As he had no heirs Whittington left his considerable fortune to charity and also supported many worthy causes in his lifetime. A list of recipients includes:

The rebuilding of Guildhall – the paving and some of the glazing – and establishing the first library at Guildhall.
Books for the Greyfriars Library.
A ward for unmarried mothers at St Thomas' Hospital.
A large public lavatory called Whittington's Longhouse, at St Martin Vintry, flushed by the Thames.
The rebuilding of Newgate Prison.
Repairing St Bartholomew's Hospital.
Installing the first public drinking fountain in the City.

There is no contemporary mention of a cat. By the seventeenth century Dick Whittington had become a popular story character, and diarist Samuel Pepys mentions seeing a stage performance about him, but nobody is sure when or why the cat appeared. There are various theories, ranging from 'cat's' derivation from a distortion of a French word 'to purchase' to a type of coal boat. Black cats are supposed to be lucky so perhaps it is just a symbol of his fortunate life.

Sir Thomas Bloodworth

Sir Thomas Bloodworth.

Sir Thomas was probably born in the early 1620s in London. His father, of Derbyshire stock, was master of the Vintners' Company. Thomas was apprenticed to a vintner but went on to work for the Levant Company and East India Company. He became an Alderman in 1658, a master of the Vintners' Company in 1659, and a Member of Parliament In 1660. He was one of the representatives of the City who asked King Charles II to return to England for the Restoration and was knighted. He was made Sheriff in 1663 and in 1665 became Lord Mayor.

On 2 September 1666 the Great Fire broke out in Thomas Farynor's baker's shop in Pudding Lane. This area was marked afterwards by the Monument to the Great Fire. Bloodworth was summoned to the scene but thought the fire was not very serious, saying 'a maid might piss it out'. He then returned to bed. Those words would come back to haunt him as the Great Fire destroyed eighty per cent of the City of London.

At the time, houses were mostly made of wood. Fires were stopped by pulling down the houses next to the one on fire, to stop the fire spreading. However Bloodworth would not authorise this, as he could then be held responsible for destroying property. As the fire spread throughout the City, Samuel Pepys encountered him. He described him in his diary as 'like a man spent, with a hankercher about his neck' and complaining that he had been up all night. He was further described as 'looking frightened out of his wits'. Eventually the King's brother, James, Duke of York, took control of fighting the fire.

Bloodworth was vilified afterwards and his conduct during the fire condemned. He never lived down his comment that 'a maid might piss it out'. He died in 1682.

John Wilkes

John Wilkes was born in Clerkenwell in 1725, the son of a distiller. He went to the University of Leiden in the Netherlands where he learned sympathy for non-conformist Protestants and religious tolerance in general. He married into a wealthy Buckinghamshire family, and although the marriage didn't last it did produce one daughter, to whom he was devoted. Allegedly not very good looking – he had a squint and a protruding jaw – he was instead a witty and charming man. He did well with the ladies and gained a reputation as both a rake and a man of culture.

He joined the Royal Society in 1749 and became High Sheriff of Buckinghamshire in 1754. In 1757 he became MP for Aylesbury, re-elected in 1761. He was also a member of Sir Francis Dashwood's notorious Hellfire Club, famous for its well-to-do rakes and hellraisers.

He became known as radical, not so much for his Parliamentary speeches but for his publications. He published *The North Briton* which attacked the King's favourite, Lord Bute, over the war with France. He also attacked William Hogarth, the painter and cartoonist, who from then on lampooned him too. He was arrested for seditious libel for an article published in *The North Briton* but kept his parliamentary seat and was later released due to parliamentary privilege. Wilkes's cause had great popular support and signs declaring 'Wilkes and Liberty' could be seen everywhere.

John Wilkes.

Unfortunately, he had written an obscene poem. It was read out in Parliament by his enemies to implicate him, and this laid him open to charges of seditious libel for his articles in *The North Briton*. It was decided his parliamentary privilege did not apply, so he fled to France and was outlawed in Britain. He spent about four years on the continent where he met, amongst others, Voltaire.

He came back to Britain and was elected to Parliament for Middlesex but was sentenced to two years in prison for his previous misdemeanours. His supporters came out to demonstrate on his behalf and some were killed in clashes with the authorities. In 1769 parliament expelled him for being an outlaw. He was re-elected and expelled again. This was repeated and Parliament finally replaced him. Lord Mayor William Beckford became involved and famously protested to King George III about Wilkes's treatment.

Wilkes became an Alderman for the City of London in 1769, Sheriff in 1771, and continued to campaign for freedom of the press. In 1774 he became Lord Mayor of London and re-entered Parliament as MP for Middlesex. He was a very popular Lord Mayor and his beloved daughter Polly became his mayoress. He held many extravagant entertainments and campaigned for the people to have more involvement in law making.

In 1779 he became Chamberlain of the City of London. As he grew older he became less popular, and less radical too, and during the Gordon Riots in 1780 he sided with the establishment. In 1784 he was elected MP for Middlesex again but did not contest the seat in 1790. He died in 1797 and there is a statue of him in Fetter Lane, EC4.

Chapter 8

The City of London Corporation and the Livery Companies

As you enter the Great Hall, at the far eastern end is a raised area known as the Dais. This is where the Lord Mayor and Aldermen sit during council meetings, because Guildhall, as well as being a historic building, is also the City of London town hall. It is where council meetings are held to deal with the day to day running of the City.

The council is called the Court of Common Council, comprising of Common Councilmen and Aldermen. It meets nine times every year and proceedings begin when an officer called the Common Cryer calls for order.

The Mayor and Aldermen sit on the Dais with the Town Clerk and the senior officers of the City of London. The Common Councilmen (many of whom are women) sit in the body of the Great Hall beneath them. At the entrance end of the Great Hall to the west sit members of the public – anyone can come in and watch the proceedings.

Above and opposite: The Great Hall prepares for Common Council.

94

The City of London is divided into twenty-five wards: Aldersgate, Aldgate, Bassishaw, Billingsgate, Bishopsgate, Bread Street, Bridge, Broad Street, Candlewick, Castle Baynard, Cheap, Coleman Street, Cordwainer, Cornhill, Cripplegate, Dowgate, Farringdon Within, Farringdon Without, Langbourn, Lime Street, Portsoken, Queenhithe, Tower, Vintry and Walbrook.

Not many people actually live in the City – about 9,000 at the time of writing. However a lot of people work there – at the time of writing about 455,000. For this reason some people who do not live in the City, but who work there, are given a vote. A sole trader and businesses up to nine employees are given one vote. A business with up to fifty staff gets one vote for every five employees. Businesses with more than fifty staff get ten votes, then one vote per fifty after that.

Common Council

The councillors are the Common Councilmen and there are one hundred of them. Their job is to ensure the smooth running of the city, like councillors everywhere. They are usually independent – the Common Council is not party political. They must be British, Commonwealth or EU citizens and Freemen of the City of London (more of this later). They must also be registered to vote on the City of London ward list or own freehold or leasehold estate in the City (in practice this could be as simple as having a nominal interest in a small office space) or have lived in the City for the previous twelve months.

Common Council
Chamber, eighteenth
century.

Common Councillors are unpaid. Each ward, depending on its size, has between two and ten councillors. They are elected by the voters in their wards every four years. They are led by the Chief Commoner, who is elected annually. Common Councillors wear ceremonial gowns of mazarine blue.

Aldermen

Above the Common Councillors are the Aldermen. Each of the twenty-five wards has an Alderman. Alderman is a very old word, dating back to the Anglo-Saxon earlderman, which means elder-man, or village elder. To qualify you have to be a British subject, a Freeman of the City of London, not be an alderman for another ward and satisfy the requirements of office of a Police and Crime Commissioner. They wear scarlet robes for ceremonial occasions such as the Lord Mayor's Show and violet robes for Common Hall.

If you put yourself forward for election it means you have aspirations to be Lord Mayor, so the workload is greater than that of a Common Councilman.

96

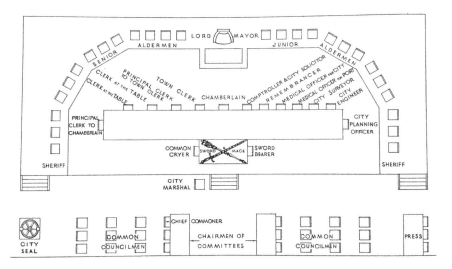

Common Council Plan, 1952.

They also have historic duties such as approving the creation of new Livery Companies and approving people for Freedom of the City. The Aldermen have their own court, which is the 'pepperpot'-like building in Guildhall Yard attached to the West Wing, with the City arms on it. They are elected every six years by the voters in their wards and must retire by the age of 70. Aldermen are also unpaid.

Sheriffs

Above the Aldermen are two Sheriffs. The office of Sheriff goes back to at least the seventh century. The Sheriffs are elected each year on Midsummer Day. They are elected by Liverymen and members of the City Livery Companies (this will be explained later). Usually one Sheriff is an Alderman, known as the Aldermanic Sheriff, and one is not, known as the Lay Sheriff.

Their main duties are to be the right-hand men of the Lord Mayor and to attend the judges at the Old Bailey where they have accommodation for the year.

Lord Mayor

Above the Sheriffs is the most important role in the City – the Lord Mayor of the City of London. To be Lord Mayor, a person must be an Alderman and have previously served as one of the two Sheriffs. They are appointed every year on Michaelmas Day, 29 September, by the Aldermen and Liverymen.

97

Other Officers of the City

The Remembrancer. This is one of the Corporation's most important officers. He is in charge of protocol. He also liaises between the Lord Mayor and the City on the one hand, and to Parliament and the Sovereign on the other.

The Recorder of London. This is the City's senior legal officer and the senior judge at the Old Bailey - the Central Criminal Court. He is a member of the Court of Aldermen but not elected. He is also the High Steward of Southwark.

The Common Serjeant. The second most senior judge at the Old Bailey, he is also the Recorder's deputy and presides over the election of the Sheriffs and Lord Mayor.

Swordbearer of London. Since the fourteenth century the Mayor has had a man to carry his sword before him. He wears a Muscovy hat and is appointed by the Court of Aldermen.

Common Cryer and Serjeant-at-Arms. The office dates from at least before 1338. He carries the Great Mace of Government before the Lord Mayor and is also appointed by the Court of Aldermen.

Common Council in session.

City Marshal. The origin of the office dates from 1595 and the office is that of the Lord Mayor's peacekeeper. He marshals civic processions and represents the Lord Mayor when privileged regiments (those allowed to march through the City) enter the City and he escorts them. He is also appointed by the Court of Aldermen.

Chamberlain of London. This role is discussed in more detail in Chapter 17, Guildhall Today.

Livery Companies

When entering the Great Hall you will see twelve banners suspended from the ceiling. There is also a frieze of coats of arms that runs around the Great Hall. These belong to the Guilds, or Livery Companies, and an understanding of the Livery Companies is important for an understanding of how the City of London works.

Guildhall, as the name might suggest, is the place where the Guilds came together.

The Guilds, or Livery Companies, started as trade associations which were founded mostly during the twelfth to fifteenth centuries. New ones are still being formed and in 2014 the Art Scholars became the 110th Worshipful Company. The earliest to receive a royal charter were the Weavers, who received their charter in 1155. The concept of organised trade associations probably goes back to the 800s, in Saxon times. As mentioned above, the name 'guild' may come from 'gield', an Old English word for 'pay tribute'.

They also had their origins in medieval religious fraternities. When the Guilds called themselves 'Worshipful Companies' it meant they worshipped together. They became known as Livery Companies because they wore different costumes or 'livery' to differentiate companies from one another and these would be worn on ceremonial occasions and in processions. By the Middle Ages the Livery Companies were an important part of the fabric of the City.

Different parts of the City were associated with different professions and trades and the effect of that can still be seen today. If you walk around Cheapside – 'cheap' means market in Anglo-Saxon and was a market area – you will still see streets with 'market' names like Wood Street, Bread Street and Milk Street, or Honey Lane and Ironmonger Lane. The people dealing in those commodities would have traded there and lived there and if you wanted their particular product, that is where you would go.

Livery Companies were not just a kind of trade union but were also regulatory, involved in setting standards and prices. They would make sure their apprentices knew their trade. They would make sure that traders did not overcharge or undercharge and they would also make sure that their members did not produce sub-standard work or sell shoddy goods. If a member did do this they would be penalised. Punishments could run from time spent in the pillory to full removal of Freeman status.

Guilds looked after their members. They supported members who fell on hard times and when they died the Company would look after the widows and orphans. They founded schools and almshouses and said prayers for deceased members. Members left bequests and property to the Livery Companies and this made them wealthy. Their wealth and their control of trade within the City made them very powerful organisations.

There were three ways to join a Livery Company. The first was by Servitude – apprenticeship. If you were accepted as an apprentice you would be bound to your master for seven years to learn the trade and make sure your work was up to the accepted standard. After your seven years you would then become a Freeman and able to trade in your own right.

The second way was through Patrimony. If your father was a Guild member you could become a member.

The third way was through Redemption. If the Company thought you could bring something to them that they wanted you could pay a fee to join.

These methods of joining still apply today, but most Companies no longer run apprenticeships. A Freeman is a junior member of a Livery Company and a senior member is called a Liveryman.

With their wealth and importance in City trade the Livery Companies had a lot of influence. They were involved in governing the City, and in appointing the Lord Mayor and they continue to do so. The Lord Mayor will be associated with a Livery Company and some are associated with several.

In the Middle Ages there was much argument between the Livery Companies, mostly over which were more important, including some street fighting and actual deaths. In 1515 it was decided to set an official Order of Precedence and the twelve most important Livery Companies, based on how many times they had provided a Lord Mayor, became known as the Great Twelve. The banners of the Great Twelve are those that can be seen suspended in the Great Hall. The Great Twelve in order of precedence are:

1. Mercers - luxury fabric and accessories
2. Grocers - originally 'pepperers' who dealt in spices
3. Drapers - woollen cloth
4. Fishmongers
5. Goldsmiths
6. Merchant Taylors - tailors
7. Skinners - fur
8. Haberdashers – ribbons, gloves, caps and hats
9. Salters - salt
10. Ironmongers
11. Vintners - wine
12. Clothworkers - cloth preparation

The Merchant Taylors and Skinners could never agree about their precedence and take it in turns every year to be numbers six or seven.

Until 1742 the Lord Mayor could only be selected from one of one of the Great Twelve, but ever since then they have been able to come from any Livery Company.

Some Companies would be based in a building known as a Livery Hall, and there are quite a few of these still around the City. The origin of 'Hallmark' on jewellery comes from their having been examined for quality and marked at Goldsmith's Hall in Foster Lane, EC2. These Halls are well worth visiting and some do open their doors for group visits or on Open House day.

The Companies would be run by a Master who would be in charge of standards and discipline. But it was not all work. There would also be banquets on festivals such as Master's Day, where large amounts of food and drink would be consumed. In the seventeenth century one Company's banquet involved many types of fish, swans, boiled tongue and udders, goose, capon, buck, asparagus, mutton, beef, apple pies and warden pies (pear). Also fourteen gallons of Canary wine, sixteen gallons of French wine and two gallons of Rhenish wine. Minstrels and musicians would provide the entertainment.

Many of the Livery Companies have their individual ceremonies and traditions. For example the dinners of some Companies feature the Ceremony of the Loving Cup. It refers back to the killing of King Edward the Martyr in 978 AD who is said to have been murdered while drinking from a horn with a large rim. This was so large it took two hands to hold, so he was off his guard and was stabbed by his enemies. This led to a ruling that horns and cups should have lids and that the person offering the vessel should lift the lid with their dagger hand. Furthermore another person should stand behind the drinker, to guard him from attack. This evolved into the Ceremony. In the Ceremony the cup is passed round the company, people taking it in turns to offer the cup and lift the lid, to drink, and to guard the drinker's back.

As the centuries have passed some of the old trades disappeared and trade and manufacturing in general moved out of the City of London. So what was the function of the Livery Companies to be? In the nineteenth century there was a re-examination of their role and a lot of them decided to concentrate on philanthropy and education, which they still do. Many chose schools and housing. Others became involved in the City and Guilds organisation.

Some were, and are, still involved in their original trades. The Goldsmiths still hallmark gold, silver and platinum items. The Fishmongers are involved in the fish industry and the Apothecaries are still involved in the pharmaceutical industry. Others have moved on with the times. The Armourers, for example, are now involved in material science.

At the time of writing there are about 26,000 Liverymen and 15,000 Freemen in the City of London – and of course there are now many Liverywomen, including two Lord Mayors. In 2010 the Livery Companies gave £42 million to charitable ventures.

Chapter 9

The Church of St Lawrence Jewry

To the south of Guildhall, on the south west corner of the Yard is the church of St Lawrence Jewry next Guildhall. It is so named because it is next to the area of the city where the Jewish community lived until their expulsion in 1290 – the Great Synagogue was situated not far away – and the church is next to Guildhall. It was the custom in the City to give churches more detailed names than usual – names such as St Mary Abchurch, St Mary-at-Hill and St Mary Woolnoth – to distinguish them one from another, as there are many churches in the city.

St Lawrence is the official church of the City of London Corporation. The Lord Mayor attends six times a year. The City coat of arms is on the internal north wall and the City flag is on the south sanctuary wall. The Lord Mayor has his own pew on the front row, as do the Sheriffs, and the Aldermen sit behind. The Lord Mayor's pew has the City coat of arms on it. Along the south aisle sit the Swordbearer, the Serjeant-at-Arms and the City Marshal. The place names are written on the pews. The decorated wrought iron construction at the front of the pews is the Lord Mayor's sword rest.

When the Lord Mayor enters the church he is preceded by his official sword and mace and they are placed in the sword rest and in front of it. Quite a few City churches still have sword rests. One of the front pews on the northern side is marked with Master of Balliol College, Oxford, patron of the living (a position as a vicar with an income) of St Lawrence from 1294 to 1954.

Church of St Lawrence Jewry, west entrance.

THE CHURCH OF ST LAWRENCE JEWRY

St Lawrence Jewry is also the church of the Livery Companies. Many Livery Companies have connections to a particular church but St Lawrence is the church of the Companies as a whole. Several of their crests can be seen in the church including the Girdlers (candle sticks), Haberdashers (above the main door), Loriners (on a prie-dieu) and Mercers (lectern). The Parish Clerks have a banner. There is also a display of different Livery Companies' collecting bags on the wall in the vestibule, featuring the Chartered Surveyors, Girdlers, Launderers, Loriners, Parish Clerks, Saddlers, Shipwrights, Wax Chandlers and Woolmen.

It has been a site of worship for many centuries and it is thought that at least three churches have stood on the site. A church was first mentioned in 1136. It originally had a church yard but that has long gone. Samuel Pepys wrote of visiting the old church on 12 February 1664. The Great Fire of London destroyed St Lawrence Jewry in 1666 and it was rebuilt by Christopher Wren and his associate Robert Hooke from 1671 to 1677. It was the most expensive City church he rebuilt, at a cost of £11,870, and one of the first. It was destroyed again on 29 December 1940 during the Blitz in the Second World War. Some cups that survived the blaze are displayed in a glass case and show the intensity of the heat. The church was restored after the war by architect Cecil Brown from 1954 to 1957.

The church has got an irregular shape to reflect the shape of the original pre-1666 church. There is a theory that this irregularity was due to the original church building being constrained by an unknown obstruction, which may have been the

Church of St Lawrence Jewry, interior.

remains of the Roman amphitheatre, which was later discovered close by. Wren varied the thickness of the walls so that the interior would be squared off. The current west wall is out of alignment with the north and south sides, but the spire is in alignment, so the spire looks at odds with the tower. The post-war steeple is made out of fibreglass.

The east side of the church is unusually ornate as it faces the main entrance into Guildhall Yard. It has five bays separated by Corinthian columns. The three centre bays project forward and are topped with a triangular pediment with a round window. The centre and outer bays have round-headed niches and the others round-headed windows. Above the windows and niches are carved fruit and flowers. There is a traditional blue police box next to the east side, which no longer works.

Church of St Lawrence Jewry, north side from Guildhall Yard.

THE CHURCH OF ST LAWRENCE JEWRY

The weathervane of 1732 is in the shape of a gridiron, which is the symbol of the martyrdom of St Lawrence. A depiction of the incendiary bomb that destroyed the church in the Blitz was later incorporated into the weathervane. St Lawrence was a third-century deacon of the Christian church in Rome. The emperor at the time was Valerian who was persecuting the Christians. In 258 AD he demanded that Pope Sixtus II should hand over all the Church's riches. The Pope refused and he was put to death. Valerian then approached Lawrence, as the Pope's deputy, and made the same demand. Lawrence instead gave what treasure the church had to the poor, then gathered some of the sick and needy of Rome and presented them to the Emperor, telling him that these were the riches of the church. For his audacity he was martyred – they roasted him to death on a gridiron. There is a story that during the ordeal he cried out, 'I am half done, turn me over!'

Post-War the church has been beautifully restored. Wren's plans for the church were still in the Guildhall archives and the white and gold ceiling has been faithfully recreated. The original windows would have been plain but now the church boasts some magnificent stained glass. The font, of 1620, was originally from Holy Trinity, Minories, and the cover incorporates wood from the old Guildhall roof.

The Commonwealth Chapel screen, surmounted by the Royal Coat of Arms of Elizabeth II, divides the nave from the Commonwealth Chapel. It is made of carved oak and incorporates the arms of the Province of Canterbury and the Diocese of London. It features a wrought iron screen which was made and presented to the church by the Royal Marines. They were affiliated to the church in 1974. The other similarly designed iron gates were donated by the Parachute Regiment and Airborne Forces in 1979.

The Tillotson Memorial Tablet is close to the altar on the North Sanctuary wall. John Tillotson (1630-94) became Dean of St Paul's Cathedral in 1689, Archbishop of Canterbury in 1691, and was a Fellow of the Royal Society. Born in Sowerby, Yorkshire and educated at Clare Hall, Cambridge he was brought up as a puritan and was known as a good practical preacher concentrating on personal morality. He preached in St Lawrence Jewry, was married there to a niece of Oliver Cromwell, and was buried in a vault beneath.

The church organ, built by Klais of Bonn in 2001, is regarded as one of the best in the country. There is another smaller one in the Commonwealth Chapel. The church also owns a Steinway concert grand piano which used to belong to Sir Thomas Beecham.

The church tower has eight bells. The original bells were destroyed in the Blitz and new ones were cast by the Whitechapel Bell Foundry in London's east end in 1957. The original bells melted in the heat and were incorporated into the new ones. The foundry was the oldest manufacturing company in the United Kingdom and had been in production since 1570 until it closed in May 2017. Its most famous bells are the Liberty Bell and Big Ben.

Windows and Paintings

There is a painting of the Martyrdom of St Lawrence in the vestibule. It survived both the Great Fire and the Blitz. It is late sixteenth century of the North Italian School.

The church has some wonderful stained-glass windows and the man responsible for most of them was Christopher Rahere Webb. He was born in 1886 and was given the uncommon middle name of Rahere because when he was born his father and his uncle, the architect Sir Aston Webb, were working on the restoration of the church of St Bartholomew the Great. It was Rahere the monk who had founded the hospital in 1123. Webb was educated at Rugby School and the Slade in London, and was then articled to Sir Ninian Comper, a Gothic Revivalist architect known for his stained glass.

The East Windows commemorate the church's patrons. On the south side is St Catherine who represents Balliol College, Oxford, patron from 1294 to 1954. On the north side St Paul represents the Dean and Chapter of St Paul's Cathedral, who were joint patrons with Balliol College from 1667 to 1954. Near the bottom of each window is an angel. St Paul's angel is holding the church without a roof, with a burning London skyline in the background, and searchlights looking for German bombers. St Catherine's angel is holding the rebuilt church, now with a roof, so these windows are also commemorating the church's restoration.

Church of St Lawrence Jewry, south windows.

There are five windows on the south side of the church. At the east end nearest the altar is a window depicting Sir Thomas More (1478-1535) who was born in Milk Street near to the church. He lectured in the church in 1501 and went on to become Chancellor of England from 1529 to 1532 under King Henry VIII. He was executed in 1535.

The next window is St Mary Magdalene. The parish of St Mary Magdalene Milk Street was combined with St Lawrence Jewry after the Great Fire. The next is St Michael. In 1892 the parish of St Michael Bassishaw was also combined with St Lawrence Jewry.

The next window is a depiction of St Lawrence himself, the church's patron saint. He is holding the gridiron, his symbol, and the palm of martyrdom – in Christian iconography the palm represents the victory of martyrs – and he is wearing a purse, because as a deacon he was responsible for looking after the early church's money.

The final window in the row is William Grocyn (1446-1519). He was vicar of St Lawrence Jewry from 1496 to 1517 and a friend of Thomas More. He studied Greek and reintroduced it to English scholarship, so that original Greek source material could be available for study. There is a quotation from Erasmus on the window saying William Grocyn was 'The patron and preceptor of us all'.

In the Commonwealth Chapel the three windows in the north side represent the Commonwealth as it was in 1957. The window on the west side has the arms of Canada, Australia, New Zealand and Malaya. The centre window depicts St George, patron saint of England, slaying the dragon. Beneath him are the symbols of the United Kingdom: a leek for Wales, thistle for Scotland, rose for England and shamrock for Ireland. The east window has the arms and flags of South Africa, India, Pakistan, Ghana and Ceylon. The window behind the altar is of Christ ascending in majesty.

Perhaps the most well-known window is in the vestibule. As you enter, turn right and look to the right above the stairs, you will see it. It depicts Sir Christopher Wren who rebuilt the church after the Great Fire of London, together with Grinling Gibbons, the famous carver of both wood and stone, and Wren's master mason Edward Strong. Gibbons is on the left and Strong on the right.

Beneath Sir Christopher are workmen, working on restoration. At the bottom of the window is a 1950s scene – Cecil Brown the architect planning the post-war restoration with the vicar, Frank Trimingham. Some of Wren's other churches feature here as well.

Sir Christopher Wren was one of this country's most famous architects. His best-known building is St Paul's Cathedral which is a short distance from St Lawrence Jewry. He is buried in the crypt of St Paul's Cathedral and above his tomb is the epitaph, *Lector, si monumentum requiris, circumspice*, 'Reader, if you seek his monument, look around you'.

Wren was born in Wiltshire in 1632, the son of a clergyman. He attended Wadham College, Oxford. Here he studied the classics but also became fascinated by the sciences. He became a Fellow of All Souls in 1653 and in 1660 became a founder member of the Royal Society. He continued his investigations into the sciences, becoming known, among a wide range of other scientific activities, for his studies in optics and astronomy. The profession of architect as such did not exist as it does today but he had an interest in it and had more or less mastered its principles by the early 1660s.

His first buildings were the chapel of Pembroke College, Cambridge and the Sheldonian Theatre, Oxford. In 1669 he became Surveyor of the Kings Works. The Great Fire had burned down eighty percent of the City and had destroyed or badly damaged eighty-seven churches as well as St Paul's Cathedral and Guildhall. Wren was in charge of replacing and repairing many of the damaged and destroyed structures. This included the Cathedral and fifty-one City churches, including St Lawrence Jewry. Most were complete by 1690 except for some of the steeples which were finished in the early eighteenth century. St Paul's Cathedral was reconsecrated in 1711, completed in Wren's lifetime, which was quite an achievement.

He went on to design a range of other famous buildings. An interesting one not far from Guildhall, on Fish Street Hill, is the Monument to the Great Fire of London which he designed with his colleague Robert Hooke. It is the tallest free-standing stone column in the world and is open to the public. Wren died aged 90 in 1723.

Grinling Gibbons (1648-1721) was a famous wood carver and sculptor, long thought of as the greatest British wood carver. He was born in Holland to an English family but emigrated to England and was seen by diarist John Evelyn working in his cottage in Deptford in 1671. Evelyn was very impressed and brought Christopher Wren and diarist Samuel Pepys to see him. He also presented Gibbons to King Charles II and he was eventually hired by the King through architect Hugh May, who was rebuilding parts of Windsor Castle. His fame grew and his work can now be seen in many other buildings including Hampton Court Palace and various churches – including St Michael Paternoster Royal, St James's Piccadilly and All Hallows by the Tower. Wren employed Gibbons to carry out significant wood and stone carving at St Paul's Cathedral. As his reputation increased, he built up a large workshop which undertook a great many commissions. He liked to work in lime wood and his carvings would often feature a 'signature' pea pod.

St Lawrence is the patron saint of chefs. There is an unsubstantiated legend that one of the treasures St Lawrence gave away to the poor was the Holy Grail. A similar epitaph to that of Sir Christopher Wren in St Paul's Cathedral can be found on the wall of the vestibule, this time for Cecil Brown.

Chapter 10

History of Guildhall Art Gallery

During the 1790s former Lord Mayor John Boydell presented Guildhall with twenty-eight paintings. Boydell explained the reasons for his gift as 'First, to show my respect to the Corporation and my fellow citizens. Secondly, to give pleasure to the public, and Foreigners in general. Thirdly, to be of service to the Artists, by showing their works to the greatest advantage; and Fourthly, for the mere purpose of pleasing myself.'

The Gallery's collection now numbers into the thousands of works, even though some were lost during the Second World War. Many works are loaned out to other art galleries and much is also archived, away from public view. Today Guildhall Art Gallery houses one of London's finest art collections, but the road to success hasn't always been easy.

The City of London's reason for establishing an art gallery during the late nineteenth century was not originally for pure artistic purposes. The great industrial cities of the north were leading the way in providing municipally-led culture for the masses. Leeds, Liverpool and Manchester had already established their own art galleries and the City felt it was being left behind.

Guildhall Art Gallery, the galleries.

The Corporation's first acquisitions had been as early as 1670, when it commissioned portraits of the twenty-two Fire Judges who sat in arbitration after the Great Fire of London. Only two of the portraits survive. More commissions followed, usually royal subjects such as portraits of King William and Queen Mary by Jan van der Vaardt, and King George II and Queen Caroline by Charles Jervas.

These, and other art works, were kept within the Guildhall buildings and not usually displayed for the public's enjoyment. Reflecting public opinion for more accessibility to the arts, the City of London Society of Artists, founded during the 1870s, petitioned the Court of Common Council in 1883 to hold a public exhibition in the old Court of Common Pleas.

Permission was given and their first show in 1884 was well attended, proving that demand was indeed high for a public art gallery in the City. Four rooms within the old Court were used to exhibit 900 works, including a drawing by Horace Jones of a bascule bridge, a proto design for the yet-to-be-built Tower Bridge.

Nevertheless, the City still wasn't totally converted to the idea of providing a permanent space devoted to art and it was only public pressure, with support from *The Times* newspaper, which convinced them otherwise. From 1885 plans developed quickly.

A Guildhall insider, Alfred Temple, was made the first Secretary to the Art Gallery. Temple had chased the job and had to take a drop in annual pay from £325 to £200, but he was enthusiastic and diligent and keen to create a successful gallery. Temple was provided gallery space within the old Courts of Common Pleas and Queen's Bench. These buildings, which stood to the east of the Porch, are almost exactly where today's Guildhall Art Gallery is sited.

By April 1886 John Singleton Copley's enormous canvas *Defeat of the Floating Batteries at Gibraltar* had been moved from the Common Council Chamber (see image on page 96) into the Gallery and in June 1886 the gallery officially opened. There was no purchase budget or exhibition programme, yet over 43,000 people visited in the first year. *Art Journal* merely described it as a 'modest little collection'.

By 1890 Henry Temple had doubled the amount of hanging space and put on the first loan exhibition of Dutch and Flemish painters. Over 100,000 people visited the show and this enabled Temple to continue his programme of loan exhibitions throughout the 1890s. It was during this period that Guildhall Art Gallery became the first art gallery to open to the public on Sundays.

During Queen Victoria's Diamond Jubilee year of 1897 another exhibition was mounted, this time with the wordy title of 'Pictures by Painters who have flourished during Her Majesty's Reign'. *Art Journal* was more enthusiastic this time, reporting that the show was a 'superb gathering of the best of the Victorian era paintings'.

As Secretary, Henry Temple had many successes, but some failures. He attracted a lot of donations and bequests which make up the core of the gallery's collection today. He also lobbied, but failed, to get Henry Tate to build his art gallery in the City. The City's loss was Pimlico's gain.

Following the First World War the Gallery entered a period of expanding its collection further. By 1925 it owned 1,040 works, with 404 on display and many others displayed in Guildhall or Mansion House. In 1936 Giles Gilbert Scott's proposal to redevelop the Guildhall site included a new and enlarged art gallery.

But from the time of the Munich Crisis in 1938 plans to relocate works were already being put into place. The Art Gallery closed in February 1939. Many of the art works were removed to Upper Westwood Quarry in Wiltshire, which also stored works from the British Museum, National Gallery and the Victoria & Albert Museum. Other works were stored in Newbury and Pangbourne in Berkshire, Bruton in Somerset and other rural locations.

Not all of the art works were removed. In a strange irony, during the bombing on 29 December 1940, the twenty-two portraits of the Fire Judges, which were being stored in the crypt, were damaged by water being used to put out the flames in the Great Hall. Ninety-eight other works were lost. On 10 May 1941 over 250 works stored in the Gallery basement were lost, again in a bombing raid.

Before the war was out, in November 1944, a decision had already been made to develop the Gallery's London collection, once peace and normality had been established. The ingathering of the dispersed works also began and in July 1946 Guildhall Art Gallery re-opened.

Due to bomb damage the Art Gallery building was a half-destroyed, one-storey wreck. The Gallery re-established itself within the carcass of the old building, which was described as a 'hastily erected barn-like structure' with a roof composed of straw and asphalt blocks. There was only 250 feet of hanging space, and no storage or offices.

But the Gallery functioned, and during the 1950s and '60s continued with its programme of loan exhibitions and the display of its permanent collection, which it rotated monthly.

Revisiting his pre-war plans, Giles Gilbert Scott made various proposals for a new art gallery, but more pressing reconstruction projects within Guildhall took priority. Richard Gilbert Scott subsequently made further proposals and it seemed like a new art gallery would be completed by 1976.

It was not until 1987 that Gilbert Scott was able to demolish the 'temporary' art gallery and rebuild the Guildhall Art Gallery we see today to the east side of his opened out Guildhall Yard. Its official reopening took place in 1999.

Bequests displayed in Guildhall Art Gallery include:

John Boydell (1720-1804), publisher and engraver, Lord Mayor in 1790, gave twenty-eight paintings to Guildhall during the 1790s, mainly historical, military and allegorical subjects, including *The Murder of Rizzio* by John Opie (1787).

William Dunnett. A City businessman who spent a lot of time in Italy building his art collection presented many works to the Gallery in 1888.

Charles Gassiott. A City wine merchant who from 1895 to 1902 gave the Art Gallery what became the core of its Victorian collection. Included: *My First Sermon* (1863) and *My Second Sermon* (1864) by John Everett Millais.

The Wakefield Collection. Charles Wakefield was an industrialist, founder of Castrol and Lord Mayor in 1915. Between 1911 and 1939 various sculptures and paintings were given to the Art Gallery, including works by Sir Peter Lely, Sir Joshua Reynolds, JMW Turner and William Holman Hunt.

Sir Matthew Smith (1879-1959). Smith was a British artist who studied and worked in France at the turn of the twentieth century and was associated with the post-Impressionists. Following injury in the First World War he began to focus more on landscapes and still lifes, becoming well known for associating with the Fauvist movement. The Gallery's collection of over 1,000 paintings, drawings and sketches was donated by his friend Mary Keene in 1974.

My Second Sermon. 1864. John Everett Millais. Permission of Guildhall Art Gallery.

Chapter 11

Guildhall Art Gallery: Paintings and Painters

The Guildhall Art Gallery collection can very broadly be divided into three: Victorian paintings are in the main upper gallery; a small donated exhibition of artist Sir Mathew Smith features in the gallery below; London related art, contemporary and temporary exhibitions in the lower levels.

Possibly the most famous picture in the gallery is *La Ghirlandata* by Dante Gabriel Rossetti. He was one of the leading lights of the Pre-Raphaelites. The Pre-Raphaelite movement was very influential in the Victorian period and several Pre-Raphaelite artists, or artists influenced by them, are represented in the main gallery.

To begin with, what does Pre-Raphaelite mean? The movement was started in 1848 by a group of young British artists who thought that British art was going in the wrong direction.

The establishment, represented by the Royal Academy, thought that art should be judged by the work of the painters of the renaissance, such as Raphael, with their particular attitude to composition and form. The Pre-Raphaelites wanted to go back to what they saw as a more honest period – before Raphael. They were influenced by medieval art and they wanted to return to being true to nature, to seeing things as they really are. They researched their subjects carefully and their pictures are often very detailed with every inch of the surface given equal treatment.

Three of the most well-known artists from the original Pre-Raphaelite Movement are represented in the Guildhall Art Gallery: William Holman Hunt (1827-1910), John Everett Millais (1829-96) and Dante Gabriel Rossetti (1828-82). Together they formed a group called the Pre-Raphaelite Brotherhood or PRB and the initials PRB would often appear on their paintings. It was not clear to outsiders what this meant and some thought it might be the mark of a dangerous, secret society! They produced a journal called *The Germ*, which helped to spread their ideas, but it didn't sell well and only lasted for four issues.

The original Pre-Raphaelite group lasted till 1853 but their influence continued and there was a second wave, which still included Rossetti. Well known figures from the second wave included William Morris (1834-96) and Edward Burne-Jones (1833-98). By the end of the century their influence had moved into furniture and stained glass and William Morris designs are still very much with us today.

Other art movements from the Victorian period represented in the Gallery are the aesthetic movement – the concept of 'art for art's sake' – orientalism and classicism.

Six Paintings from the Art Gallery

La Ghirlandata. Permission of Guildhall Art Gallery.

La Ghirlandata. 1873. Dante Gabriel Rossetti.

This is probably the most famous painting in the Gallery. The title means 'The Lady with Garlands' and Rossetti also designed the frame. The model is Alexa Wilding, who often worked with him. It's a good example of the long-necked and luscious-lipped portrayals of women Rossetti was painting during this period. It was painted at Kelmscott Manor and the angels were modelled by May Morris, William Morris's younger daughter. The meaning might be that this beautiful woman, playing her harp and surrounded by symbols of romance and love, roses and honeysuckle, is worthy of celestial appreciation.

But there is also an underlying touch of melancholy, the deep green flowers in the foreground suggesting the transience of beauty.

My First Sermon. 1863. Sir John Everett Millais.
The model for this painting was the artist's daughter Effie and the setting is a high-backed pew in All Saints Church in Kingston upon Thames. Effie can be seen as attentive and respectful. In 1864 Millais painted *My Second Sermon* in which the little girl has fallen asleep – no longer fascinated by the new experience. The Archbishop of Canterbury observed that it was a warning against long dull sermons.

The Music Lesson. 1877. Frederic, Lord Leighton.
The instrument featured is the *saz* from Turkey. The costumes and architecture are probably based on Leighton's observations on a journey to Damascus and the picture could be seen as 'orientalist'. The younger girl is Connie Gilchrist, who went on to become a well-known actress.

114

Right: My First Sermon. Permission of Guildhall Art Gallery.

Below: The Music Lesson. Permission of Guildhall Art Gallery.

The Eve of St Agnes. 1848. William Holman Hunt.
This is based on a poem by John Keats. According to folk legend a girl will dream of her future husband on the Eve of St Agnes. Madeline dreams of her lover Porphyro, who is an enemy of her family. While her family are feasting (seen in the background) the real Porphyro manages to find his way into her room and they escape together. It is thought that Millais painted some of the background of the picture as he and Holman Hunt shared a studio.

Sir Hugh Wyndham, Kt Judge of the Common Pleas. 1670. John Michael Wright.
This painting is otherwise known as *The Fire Judge*. After the Great Fire of London when most of the city was destroyed, a group of twenty-two 'fire judges' were appointed to sit in judgement over claims for compensation, land and property disputes. Sir Hugh Wyndham was one of them. In 1670 the Court of Aldermen commissioned a group of portraits of the judges but twenty were destroyed in the Second World War. There are only two portraits left in the gallery collection.

Defeat of the Floating Batteries at Gibraltar. 1783-91. John Singleton Copley.
This large painting concerns the Great Siege of Gibraltar (1779-83) when a British garrison of 5,000 repulsed a Spanish and French force of 65,000. The turning point of the siege came when the British fired red-hot shot into the besieging ships and set them alight, which we see in the painting. The painting took eight years to complete and the artist installed it in a tent in Green Park and charged admission to see it to help pay for the cost. It had first hung in the old Common Council Chamber

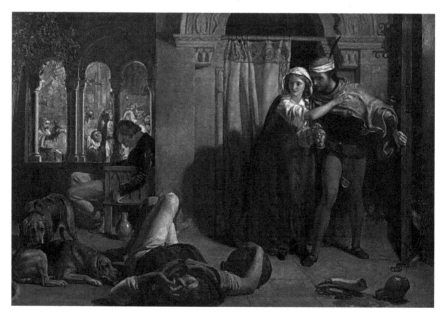

The Eve of St Agnes. Permission of Guildhall Art Gallery.

116

before being moved to the new Art Gallery in 1886. It was put in storage during the Second World War and later restored. A permanent space was found for it in the new Guildhall Art Gallery in 1999 where a double-height wall had been designed especially for it.

Right: Sir Hugh Wyndham. Permission of Guildhall Art Gallery.

Below: Defeat of the Floating Batteries at Gibraltar. Permission of Guildhall Art Gallery.

Four Artists from the Art Gallery

Dante Gabriel Rossetti was born in London in 1828. His father was Italian and taught Italian at Kings College, London. Although he had an Italian heritage Rossetti never visited Italy. As a teenager he attended the well regarded Henry Sass's drawing academy in Bloomsbury and then the Royal Academy. Widely read, he also became a published poet. In 1848 he formed the Pre-Raphaelite Brotherhood with his brother William Michael Rossetti, James Collinson, William Holman Hunt, John Everett Millais, Frederick Stephens and Thomas Woolner.

Rossetti did not like exhibiting and most of his work was sold through private commissions. In 1850 he became involved with Elizabeth 'Lizzie' Siddal, who modelled for one of his friends and then for him, and they eventually married in 1860. The art critic and social thinker John Ruskin established his Working Men's' College in Red Lion Square in 1854 and Rossetti taught painting and drawing there.

In 1856 he met William Morris and later Morris's future wife Jane Burden. Jane also sat for Rossetti. He liked painting beautiful women and it was he who gave us the word 'stunners'.

From 1861 he became involved with William Morris's Arts and Crafts firm Morris, Marshall, Faulkner and Co and was very productive during this time. Overshadowing this period was the death of his wife Elizabeth, who died from an overdose of laudanum in 1862, shortly after giving birth to a stillborn child. In his grief and in tribute he put his poems in her coffin for her burial in Highgate Cemetery.

By the mid-1860s Rossetti's health was beginning to deteriorate. He was also becoming infatuated with Jane Morris, William Morris's wife, whom he continued to paint.

He decided to publish a volume of his poems in 1870. Some had been buried with his wife, Elizabeth, so he had her exhumed in order to retrieve the poems. A hostile review of some of these later poems, regarded by many as too erotic, led to a breakdown and possibly also to a suicide attempt.

Rossetti however recovered and continued to work. He moved to Kelmscott Manor in Oxfordshire in 1873, a place which he and Morris co-rented and where he had stayed before. Jane visited him there and it was during this period that he painted *La Ghirlandata*. By now addicted to the sedative drug chloral, he overdosed in 1879. By 1882 he seemed weak and depressed and died visiting a friend in Birchington, Kent, aged 53.

Sir John Everett Millais was born in 1829 in Southampton. His father, a comfortably off gentleman, was originally from Jersey. Like Rossetti, Millais went to Henry Sass's academy and aged only 11 was admitted to the Royal Academy Schools. He was their youngest ever student and was known as a prodigy.

He became friends with William Holman Hunt and the meeting that led to the formation of the Brotherhood in 1848 took place in Millais' house. Millais' reputation grew and he was elected an associate of the Royal Academy in 1853. The critic John Ruskin and his wife Effie became friends with Millais. But Effie and Millais fell in love and she left Ruskin on the grounds of non-consummation of their marriage. Millais and Effie were married in 1855 and they would go on to have eight children.

In 1856 Millais' works began selling as engravings, increasing his reputation and his income. His art became ever more popular in the 1850s and '60s and he was working with major art dealers. He also became involved in book and magazine illustration. At first living in Perth, Millais and Effie returned to London in 1861. Millais began painting children around this time, often using his own children as models. *My First Sermon*, using his daughter Effie as the model, is a famous example. This painting helped with his election to the Royal Academy in 1863.

In the 1860s his style started to show the influence of the old masters, in contrast to his earlier Pre-Raphaelite beliefs. He was also becoming intrigued by the work of the aesthetic movement, including James Whistler. Success continued as a celebrity portraitist, and his child portraits also continued, most famously when his grandson, Willie James, modelled for a picture called *Bubbles* which was later used for an advertisement by Pears Soap. He was made Baronet in 1885.

On 20 February 1896 he was elected president of the Royal Academy, although he was ill with cancer of the larynx and he died on 13 August 1896 aged 67. He is buried in the crypt of St Paul's Cathedral in Artists' Corner near to the artist J.M.W. Turner.

William Holman Hunt was born in 1827, close to Guildhall in Cheapside, in the City of London, son of William Hunt, a warehouseman and his wife Sarah. He liked to draw from an early age, but his father did not want him to be a painter and in 1839 decided that William should leave school and go to work. He did, but he studied art in the evenings. He painted some portraits, one of which was so good that his father decided to encourage him after all.

In the summer of 1844 he met the young painter Millais who encouraged him to apply to the Royal Academy Schools again (he had tried and failed before) and this time he was accepted and became a full student in December.

His painting *The Eve of St Agnes* was in the Royal Academy Exhibition of 1848 and was much admired by Dante Gabriel Rossetti. The two became friends, shared a studio, and with Millais became part of the Pre-Raphaelite Brotherhood.

Hunt's work continued to develop, based on concepts that he had carefully thought through before starting out on them, and he became religious. In 1851 he began *The Light of the World* which became his most famous religious painting. It was exhibited at the Royal Academy in 1854. Two more versions were later painted.

In the summer of 1852 he painted what was probably his greatest landscape, known as *Strayed Sheep*. Shown in the 1853 Royal Academy Exhibition it impressed Thomas Fairbain, an engineer, who decided to give Hunt an unlimited commission.

Hunt also travelled to the Middle East, which affected his religious soul deeply. *The Scapegoat*, painted at the Dead Sea, was admired at the Royal Academy Exhibition and, reflecting his growing reputation, sold for a high price.

His 1860 painting *The Finding of the Saviour in the Temple* sold for £5,500, a record price for a contemporary painting. A queue for the gallery exhibition of the painting jammed Bond Street. In 1865 he married Fanny Waugh. They settled in Florence and here Fanny died shortly after giving birth to their son. Hunt was heartbroken and returned to London.

Between 1869 and 1892 he returned to Jerusalem several times and produced more religious works. In 1875 he married Edith, his wife's younger sister, which was prohibited at the time. They went on to have two children, who would pose for him, as did Edith.

Infuriated that people had to pay to see the original *Light of the World*, at Keble College Oxford, Hunt painted the third version. His last oil painting, it was bought by wealthy ship owner and sociologist Charles Booth who paid for it to travel the world and to be seen by millions. It is now on permanent display in St Paul's Cathedral. In 1905 he was awarded the Order of Merit and an honorary Doctorate from Oxford University. He died in 1910 and his cremated remains lie buried in the crypt of St Paul's Cathedral near to the painter J.M.W. Turner.

Frederic Lord Leighton was born in 1830 in Scarborough. With his father Dr Frederic Leighton and mother Augusta he moved to London during the early 1830s. Although he attended University College School from the age of 8, most of his childhood and early adulthood was spent travelling Europe and he had art lessons in various different academies.

In 1851 Leighton visited London to see the Great Exhibition and to meet other artists. He then went to Rome where he took a studio. Burgeoning success came in 1855 when he sent paintings to the Royal Academy in London. *Cimabue's Madonna Carried in Procession through the Streets of Florence* was bought by Queen Victoria.

The same year he moved to Paris and met other artists among whom the concept of 'art for art's sake' was emerging. Two of his paintings were shown at the Royal Academy in 1859 and this time the Prince of Wales bought one.

He was by no means established fully yet. His work was of the 'aesthetic' type which was new to Britain. He first attempted election as an associate of the Royal Academy in 1861 but was not elected until 1864. He became a member in 1868 and the exhibition of 1869 saw several of his works on display – together with those of other artists whose work he approved. He was by now on the hanging committee and becoming more influential.

In the late 1860s and early 1870s he travelled to Spain, Constantinople, Turkey, Greece, Venice, Egypt and Damascus, with a concentration on landscape painting. He was also a sculptor, although not prolific.

In 1878 he was elected President of the Royal Academy and was knighted. He made reforms in the running of the Royal Academy Schools and was an energetic champion of the arts. Many society receptions were held at his distinctive Holland Park house in Kensington, which is now open to the public.

His final works were concerned with themes of life, death and rebirth, such as *Flaming June*, his final masterpiece. He had an angina attack in 1894 and went to North Africa to convalesce. When he returned he resigned as President of the Royal Academy.

As a final honour he was given a peerage in the New Year's Honours List of 1896. On 24 January 1896 the patent creating him Baron Leighton of Stretton was issued, but he died the next day. He is buried in the crypt of St Paul's Cathedral, near to the painter JMW Turner.

Chapter 12

The Roman Amphitheatre

The remains of the amphitheatre are underneath the Art Gallery on the east side of Guildhall Yard. Roman remains are usually found about twenty feet under modern London. There is not a large amount left visible of the amphitheatre – just some remains of the East Gate, a small section of the lower parts of the wall, some of the drainage system, and sand which was used in the arena. Clever techniques incorporating lighting and luminescent effects have recreated the atmosphere of what the amphitheatre may have been like, including figures of combatants.

The floor has stainless steel markings to show where the drains ran and there is a brass mark at the entrance to show where a large threshold made out of timber was found. On the surface of Guildhall Yard there is a ring of dark paving marking the line of where the amphitheatre walls would have been.

The amphitheatre was elliptical and roughly the size of a modern football pitch. The Romans reputedly kept their citizens happy with bread and circuses

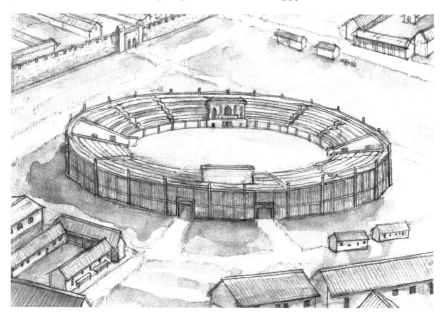

Roman Amphitheatre, Londinium.

and the amphitheatre was the setting for the circuses. The Colosseum in Rome was built under the Emperor Vespasian (AD 69-79) and other amphitheatres soon appeared throughout the Empire. The amphitheatres were built with public money but individuals, often emperors, staged the games to increase their own popularity. Everyone was allowed to go to the games, men and women, and admission was free.

Amphitheatres were used, broadly speaking, for three types of activity: the execution and torture of criminals, prisoners of war and occasionally Christians; the hunting and baiting of animals; and gladiatorial combat – fights to the death between gladiators. In the Roman Colosseum games could go on for several days and thousands of animals and humans died. Amphitheatres were also sometimes used for religious purposes. The London amphitheatre was close to the Roman fort, near to the wall, and might have been used for military exercises as well.

Animals used in the Colosseum in Rome included exotic beasts such as lions and leopards, but the London amphitheatre would have used bears, boars, wolves and bulls which would have been a lot cheaper and easier to bring in. They would either have matched the animals against each other, or they would have been matched against *venatores*, men who had been specially trained to fight animals – a different training to that of a gladiator. There would probably have been more wild beast fights than gladiatorial combats as gladiators were expensive to train.

The name gladiator comes from the Latin for sword, which is gladius. Gladiatorial combat started in the fourth century BC as part of funeral rituals and the first recorded public showing was in 264 BC in Rome. Combats became part of the official games to celebrate religious festivals in the first century BC and permanent arenas were first constructed at around this time. At the time of the London amphitheatre there would have been different types of gladiator. Examples would be the *secutor*, who was armed with a short sword, a shield and leg armour, or the *retiarius* who would have a net, a trident, shoulder armour and a dagger.

Some gladiators were volunteers, usually the poor who wanted a way out of their condition. Others were condemned to the arena as criminals, to be released after a certain time if they survived. They were trained up by instructors called *lanistae*, who were usually ex-gladiators themselves. The death rate among gladiators was, not surprisingly, high. Sometimes a particularly successful gladiator who managed to survive would be rewarded with his freedom. Some even became celebrities. Gladiatorial combat in the Roman Empire continued to the end of the fourth century and probably ended in Britain in the third century.

When a gladiator defeated an opponent, but had not killed him, it was customary for him to ask whoever had commissioned the games to decide on the loser's fate. It has long been assumed this was done by giving the thumbs up or thumbs down sign. The decision was often influenced by the roars of the crowd.

So how was the Londinium amphitheatre discovered? Archaeologists knew that Roman Londinium had been a sizable settlement and should have had an amphitheatre but they had not managed to find evidence of one. The original

Guildhall Art Gallery was established in 1886 on the east side of the Yard. It had been badly bombed in the Second World War and in 1987 it was decided to knock it down and build a new one. During the redevelopment archaeologists were brought in to see if they could find anything of interest on the site – and in 1988 among other things they found the amphitheatre, which they knew must have existed somewhere. It was described in *The Observer* as 'one of the most exciting archaeological finds since the Second World War'. It was the first major excavation of the Museum of London Archaeological Service. After a pause in work to redesign the art gallery the excavation continued in 1992. The art gallery was redesigned to incorporate the newly exposed amphitheatre and it was finally opened in 1999.

Part of the stone amphitheatre is on the first basement level of the gallery and to incorporate it, the design required a very challenging piece of engineering. It began in 1994. The design had to be changed to keep the Roman remains where they were and at the same time accessible to the public. The design of the two sub-basements below the amphitheatre had to be altered due to the extra – and unexpected – weight of the Roman remains. The amphitheatre was opened to the public in 2002. Work on the Roman drains continued separately and they were added in 2006.

The first amphitheatre built in Roman Londinium was constructed in AD 74 and was made out of wood. There is a theory that it was built for the fort as it was very close by. It was about 285 feet long and 243 feet across. It would have seated up to seven thousand spectators, the population of Londinium then estimated at about twenty thousand. There was a wooden wall around it and there were large entrances at the eastern and western ends. There were probably two smaller entrances in the southern side which may have come together once you were inside. The eastern gate was large – over sixteen feet wide. There would have been stands for the dignitaries to sit in at the north and southern sides.

The Amphitheatre beneath the Guildhall Art Gallery.

THE ROMAN AMPHITHEATRE

Around the time of Emperor Hadrian's visit to Britannia, in AD 122, it was rebuilt, partly in stone – they used Kentish ragstone – and slightly enlarged. The new stone sections included the walls round the arena and the areas around the entrances. There were chambers on either side of the eastern entrance, which may have been used as resting rooms or as shrines to make offerings before a contest. Or they could have been used to pen wild animals before they were released into the arena.

The stone walls were up to eight feet high then topped off with timber. The new amphitheatre had more rows of seating and could probably hold from 7,000 to 10,500 spectators. The surface was of gravel topped with sand. It would probably have had plastered walls which would have been brightly painted. Fragments of marble and Egyptian and Greek porphyry were found on the site, which may have come from the dignitaries' seating area.

Because of its location the amphitheatre needed good drainage. There were wooden drains running around the arena and the east entrance, which ran off into the River Walbrook. Much of the system was preserved and you can see some of it in the exhibited remains.

The Romans left Britannia and Londinium in AD 410, primarily to help prevent Rome being attacked. It's believed the amphitheatre had already been abandoned during the fourth century AD. The area became waterlogged. By AD 367 the masonry was being removed to be used elsewhere, perhaps to prop up the defences against the early Saxon invaders. The area might also have been used as a dump, possibly an official one. Eventually over the years the amphitheatre area was reclaimed by nature.

Some interesting objects were found during the amphitheatre excavations. These included some curse tablets – these are tablets naming someone who has done you wrong, stolen something from you for example, and cursed by you with the help of a god. The god receives part of the stolen goods as a payment. Other tablets sought to bring about the defeat of particular fighters.

One figurine found, made of lead, was probably of the goddess Juno, which may have been used to ask her for protection. There was also a gold necklace clasp, a brooch and carved bone hairpins that had been lost by women in the audience, and also some oddments that may have been lost by soldiers. Near the eastern entrance was what appeared to be a rubbish dump, full of broken glass and pottery.

After the Romans left, the entire Londinium area was abandoned. When the Saxons settled in London they used an area further to the west, where the Strand is now, which was called Lundenwic. The Saxons did not properly move into the old Roman part until towards the end of the ninth century, by which time the site of the amphitheatre had become overgrown and unrecognisable.

Chapter 13

Sculptures: Exterior

Dick Whittington and his Cat

Sculptor: Lawrence Tindall, 1999.
Portland stone. 4' high.

This partly obscured statue is positioned in Guildhall Yard, outside the Art Gallery
and against the wall of the Great Hall under the loggia. It features Dick Whittington

*Dick Whittington and
his Cat.*

with his cat at the Highgate mile stone. He turns his head at the sound of Bow Bells, pondering whether he should return to London. This statue was commissioned for the opening of the Art Gallery in 1999.

Busts of Samuel Pepys, Oliver Cromwell, William Shakespeare, Sir Christopher Wren.

Sculptor: Tim Crawley, 1999.
Portland stone. 4' high.

Also commissioned for the opening of Guildhall Art Gallery in 1999. These huge quarter-sized busts are positioned in niches against the Art Gallery wall underneath the loggia.

There is an interview with sculptor Tim Crawley at the end of this chapter.

Above left: Samuel Pepys.

Above right: Oliver Cromwell.

Above left: William Shakespeare.

Above right: Christopher Wren.

Glass Fountain

Sculptor: Allen David, 1969.
Glass laminae, slate, York stone. 12' high.

This sculptural fountain stands close to the North Wing on the north-west side of the piazza on Aldermansbury. Its central feature is a glass pillar surmounted by a disc, with a segment cut out. At the sculpture's base is a cluster of smaller glass sculptures of varying sizes. There are nineteen outlet points so that water cascades over the whole surface. The glass elements are held together by silicone and tensol glue.

Glass Fountain was a gift presented by Mrs Gilbert Edgar, wife of the chairman of H. Samuel who had served as a Sheriff of the City of London. She wanted to make a gift to the City and simply liked the artist and his work. It is one of the City's earliest abstract public sculptures. When installed it was a contemporary mirror to the Gothic Revivalist drinking fountain in Guildhall Yard, which would shortly be removed to make way for the new West Wing.

Born in 1926 and raised in Bombay, Allen David is an Australian artist and public commissions of his work can also be seen in Melbourne and Tel Aviv.

Glass Fountain.

Beyond Tomorrow

Sculptor: Karin Jonzen, 1972.
Bronze, York stone, concrete. 4' high x 10' long.

Positioned outside the North Wing entrance this sculpture of male and female figures reclining was intended to sit outside the adjacent City of London Exhibition Hall – a space which was barely used and soon closed.

Jonzen had also sculpted for the 1951 Festival of Britain and the themes of health and optimism are continued here. It was donated by Lord Blackford, chairman of Guardian Assurance. Jonzen disliked the first casting and paid for this second casting herself, but it was such an obvious improvement Lord Blackford paid again.

Karin Jonzen also sculpted *The Gardener* in 1971. This is a small but much-loved statue which has been moved around, but was last seen outside Brewers' Hall near London Wall.

Above: Beyond Tomorrow.

Below: Queen Elizabeth I, Queen Anne and Queen Victoria.

Queen Elizabeth I, Queen Anne and Queen Victoria.

Sculptor: J.W. Seale, 1873.
Bath stone. 6' high.

Three statues positioned in niches against the exterior wall of the old library, on the east side of Guildhall in Basinghall Street. The statues are considered to be an afterthought. Horace Jones's drawings originally featured male statues. Seale also carved the heads of the Great Men over the spandrels within the interior of Jones's Library (see page 72).

Interview with Tim Crawley – stone carver of the Guildhall Art Gallery busts

In front of the Art Gallery on the east side of Guildhall Yard are four large stone busts, in niches, of Sir Christopher Wren, Oliver Cromwell, Samuel Pepys and William Shakespeare. These were carved in Portland stone by sculptor Tim Crawley in 1998. We went to see him to talk about the sculptures, his work in general and what it is like to be a stone carver in the twenty-first century.

Tim Crawley's workshop is in some farm buildings in the countryside not far from Cambridge. Large slabs of stone can be seen outside together with an impressive carved figure of Atlas holding up the world guarding the door. The workshop itself is fascinating with traditional chisels and more modern stone-cutting equipment. Finished work and work in progress are very much in evidence. We had the interview in what he calls the mess room, where there is a table and a few chairs – if there is a large job to do, there can be quite a few sculptors drinking tea together there.

Guildhall. How did you become a sculptor?

Tim Crawley. I studied art history at Manchester University and my speciality was medieval architecture. Before I went to university I thought about going to art school but I was talked out of it. So when I finished my degree I went to art school then instead. I didn't want to be an academic. I wanted to do something practical. I thought of becoming a stone mason which fitted in with my interest in medieval architecture but I was over-qualified to get an apprenticeship or any kind of training. People wouldn't look at me. I was too old at 21!

G. Really?

TC. Oh yes. They prefer to take people at 16. Personally, I experienced a kind of prejudice against my university education, which I suppose is understandable.

Then I found out about a course at the City and Guilds of London Art School doing wood and stone carving. I went for a visit and when I saw what they were doing there I thought – this is what I want to do! I worked as a bus conductor for a year to save some money to pay the fees and then embarked on the three-year course doing wood and stone carving and conservation. I became self-employed after that. The City and Guilds of London Art School is a wonderful institution. It is very little known. It's very small and independent. It's still there and I am now running the carving department – I'm head of department! So I've gone back! I've been there for six years. And I still work as a carver as well.

G. When most people think about sculptors these days they think of arty abstract works whereas your interest is figurative. Is there a reason?

TC. I never set out to be a sculptor. I am a stone carver. And there is a distinction. My interest is historical. They are very different. I wanted to work on old buildings. I have a love of stone. I couldn't access the masonry world – so I became a carver. The difference is that a mason works architectural mouldings in stone and to a template. A stone carver will do the ornamental stuff – the bosses, foliage work, and occasionally statuary if he's lucky. So I set out to be an architectural carver if you like, and I was fortunate – these opportunities came up to do figurative work and I ended up doing quite a lot of it so I did become

Tim Crawley in his studio.

132

a sculptor. I was actually designing things to go on buildings. New work but in period style to go on historic locations. So I was working as an artist, as the design element is the difference between a sculptor and a carver.

G. Can you tell us about some of your better known works – or works on famous buildings?

TC. Here's a high profile one – there are twenty statues on the West Front of Westminster Abbey. I designed, or had a hand in designing, all of them. And I carved ten of them myself. The ten modern martyrs. That was in 1998 – there was a lot of media coverage at the time. There is also St George's Bloomsbury. I did the lions and unicorns on the base of the spire. They were taken down in 1871 and I reinstated them in 2006. That was a big commission. That building is very significant historically. I have done heraldic work for the West Door of King's College Chapel. I made a new marble Elizabethan fountain for Kenilworth Castle. And heraldic carvings for Temple Bar which is now near St Paul's.

G Which of your sculptures are you most proud of?

TC. I think probably the St George's Bloomsbury project. Each job has different aspects that you are proud of but that one was such an enormous and complex job. It was incredibly tricky to get it done. But every job is a challenge and every job is different. But the lions and unicorns are twelve feet high and they are built into the structure of the spire!

G. Let's move to the Guildhall sculptures – how were you commissioned for them?

TC. There are five niches – the main four on the face of the gallery, and then another one at the end of the loggia with a statue of Dick Whittington. I was engaged to do the main four on the gallery face. I had just finished the Abbey work – so maybe that was one commission that arose from it. The art gallery architect Richard Gilbert Scott approached me and asked me if I would do it. It was another job with a very short time span – it had to be done within a few months.

G. So they decided who the figures were going to be of. Do they decide on the size of them as well?

TC. That was my decision. I knew they had to be on a large scale to have any presence. You know how large the niche is going to be so the artistic decision is how large should a statue be within that niche. In the case of Guildhall there was a pre-existing niche and pedestal – so that was the frame I had to work with.

So I made a mock-up of the niche and made a model within it. I would do that on a small scale and then show it to the client to get approval. So the decision is what I think looks right in that space.

G. How do you decide what stone to use?

TC. In the case of Guildhall it had to be Portland Stone. Often the client will decide what stone they want but I may go to the quarry and decide which particular piece I would like to work with. Most of London is built of Portland stone.

G. Is there a particular stone you like to work with?

TC. I think Portland. Or a statuary marble. That's the white marble from Italy. Carrara marble. There are endless varieties. The one I like is a particular kind that has a translucency to it which Michelangelo used for his sculpture. It's a kind of creamy colour, not brilliant white. It's very fine grained so it will take any amount of detail. It's the most exquisite material – if you can find it! It is very difficult to find a large pure block. Often they will have veins running through them. And if you do find some it will cost a lot of money.

G. How do you buy it?

TC. You buy it by the cubic foot. You need to go to Italy and select it personally.

G. How much does stone cost?

TC. Portland stone will cost around £85 a cubic foot, sawn. So a cubic metre is about £2,200. Marble is probably three or four times that price.

G. When you are not working from a live model, but you are working from a picture, Shakespeare for example, how do you work from someone two dimensional and make it three dimensional if you can't see them?

TC. Research. You start by looking for visual evidence. If we take the case of Shakespeare there are several portraits, although none are fully authenticated. The Chandos is the most famous. And there is an effigy in Stratford. I do a lot of research before I start the job. I get as many pictures of the subject as possible before making a model which I will then show the client along with a report summarising my research. Obviously I use my imagination a bit as well! But when anyone thinks of Shakespeare they think bald head, beard – so those are sort of signals the character sends out. There are lots of pictures of Cromwell and there are carvings as well, some from life. And there is a death mask. There are four good portraits of Pepys and lots of Wren as well.

G. But even if there are pre-existing sculptures, how do you transfer a 2D image to 3D?

TC. Essentially modelling and drawing. You have to have an eye and know what to look for. If you are working on a bust – like the ones we are talking about – the key thing is the profile. If you get the profile right then things will start to fall into place around that. If you are doing a sculpture of a living individual you can take measurements with a pair of callipers. There are critical measurements that you take. But when you put it all together to make a model… it's coordinating everything together in space if you like.

G. What is the process you go through when making the actual sculpture? After you have researched the picture?

TC. The first model is made out of clay. There are drawings as well. If it's a three-dimensional sculpture the model is more important. If it's a relief the drawings are more important. Once the sketch model is approved I do a full-size model in clay. When that is approved I make a mould and cast it in plaster. The plaster version is what I use as the basis for the stone carving. Historically there are two approaches to carving – there is direct carving where you go straight to the stone and you don't have a model. It was used by primitive societies and also came back into vogue in the early twentieth century. Henry Moore was an example of a direct carver. In the system that I use for this type of work I make a model and transfer that into stone. You measure from the model. I use a pointing machine. It's not an actual machine, it is a device that finds points in space. You attach it to the model and it has a moveable pointer that you can move in and out and that will take your measurements for you. You would start from the high point of the nose for example and that will tell you how far into the block of stone that point in space should be.
    I can then drill down to fix that point. I then clear away the stone around it. And so on. You can also do the same thing using callipers.

G. Do you still use the traditional hammer and chisel?

TC. Yes we still use them but there are new innovations as well, such as the air hammer, which drives the chisel, a bit like a piston.

G. I suppose everyone asks – if you have made a wonderful sculpture and you're on the point of finishing it, what happens if you slip and take a chip out of it?

TC. You're right, everyone does ask that and I'm afraid we sculptors do not reveal the answer – it remains part of our mystery! But I can say that if you are going to make a mistake you usually make it at the beginning, not at the end. By the end of the process you are chiselling very delicately but at the beginning you are really laying into it and that may be when a mistake occurs. You might hit a flaw in the stone for example. It's all something you learn. And the longer you do it the less mistakes you make.

G. Do you see yourselves as part of the art world or the architecture world?

TC. I think we fall between two stools, as carvers. We are not masons – but we *are* craftsmen – artisans – we are that, but we are also something else. We have to be able to draw and that sets us apart from a mason. A mason will use a template. A carver draws with a chisel. So in that way we are moving into the art area. You bring something into being – you create something new, if you like, and that's where the art element comes into play. But I always work to commission, for someone else. I'm an architectural sculptor, whereas an artist is usually – artistically – working for themselves.

G. Is there any particular sculptor that you admire?

TC. I can't single out any particular one – all I can say is, all the greats! I suppose my first influence was from the medieval sculptors, as I come from Canterbury. I worked in the cathedral gift shop for a while when I was at school and I would wander round looking at the architecture and the statues. I really admire twelfth and thirteenth century Gothic carving and the really good stuff is exquisite.

G. Why do you like the medieval sculpture so much?

TC. I studied medieval architecture at university and at that point it all seemed rather similar. But when I learned to carve I saw it all with new eyes. I could see it for what it was and understand it. You can see things as a maker that you can't see as an academic. Some academics might appreciate it to a significant degree but I think that until you have done it and worked with the tools you will not have the same level of appreciation. You get an extra insight.

G. It must be a great feeling to see the figure appearing out of the stone.

TC. It's a complex experience. To begin with it can look ugly, and one can become discouraged. But then as it starts to take shape it's very different as you take fewer measurements and start to rely on your eye. It's like drawing – you can get different textures – but it's three dimensional. That's when it gets really exciting. But ultimately, there's always a feeling that you could have done better and then you start seeking out the next challenge.

Chapter 14

City of London Police Museum

City of London Police are not to be confused with the Metropolitan Police – the 'Met', who look after Greater London – they are a separate entity. The City of London Police have been responsible for policing the Square Mile since 1839. Instead of having black and white checks on their uniforms they are red and white (the colours of the City of London) and they have the arms of the City of London on their helmets instead of the Met's silver Brunswick Star.

There are three police stations in the City, at Snow Hill, Bishopsgate and Wood Street which is their headquarters. They number about 700 officers and they are the smallest force in England and Wales. Because they are based in the City they specialise in white-collar crime and fraud.

City of London Police
Museum entrance.

The museum started in the way that a lot of museums do, as the private collection of a City Police officer which slowly grew. The museum used to be in the Wood Street police station but it moved to Guildhall in 2016.

What follows is a summary and guide through highlights of the museum. As you go in you are faced with the constable's oath:

I, NAME OF OFFICER, of the City of London Police, do solemnly and sincerely declare and affirm that I will well and truly serve the Queen in the office of constable, with fairness, integrity, diligence and impartiality, upholding fundamental human rights and according equal respect to all people; and that I will, to the best of my power, cause the peace to be kept and preserved and prevent all offences against people and property; and that while I continue to hold the said office I will to the best of my skill and knowledge discharge all the duties thereof faithfully according to law.

Origins

The first area in the museum deals with policing before 1839. Well before 1839 the City was policed in different ways. By 1550 the City was divided into different areas, or wards, and men from each ward would act as watchmen (who before the thirteenth century defended the City from outside attack). It was known as the 'watch and ward' system. They were unpaid and badly trained and over time other systems were tried including a City Day Police, created in 1784, who were paid.

The watchmen would serve for one year. The City of London's wards were supervised by Aldermen who made sure that the men in their ward took their turn. The City of London's wards still have Aldermen in charge now but much of the administration is carried out by the Court of Common Council. The watch and ward system lasted until the nineteenth century.

In 1663 a new Act was passed ensuring that a thousand men should be on duty every night. They were often old and badly equipped and a source of ridicule. They were known as Charleys. In 1737 another Act allowed the Court of Aldermen to employ two marshals and six marshalmen to oversee additional men, recruited when necessary to patrol at night. The marshals checked that the constables and watchmen were on duty.

On display is a map of the pre-1839 wards, a case featuring the Marshalmens' swords and a watchman's rattle – used to call for help – a watch-house day report from 1833 and a truncheon, paid for by the Worshipful Company of Bakers.

The next area covers Victorian and Edwardian policing, where there is a list of commissioners and stations and a map of the beats and boundaries.

The Metropolitan Police were formed in 1829 to cover all of London but the City did not join it, not wanting to lose their independence and police powers. The

Police origins.

City Police were officially formed in 1839 by an Act of Parliament. The Court of Common Council created the role of Commissioner and a Police Committee who are still in charge of running the force.

Jack the Ripper

The museum has a section on Catherine Eddowes, fourth victim of Jack the Ripper, as her body was found within the City boundaries. She was known as Kate, came to London from Wolverhampton and was probably a prostitute. She lodged at Cooney's lodging house at 55 Flower and Dean Street, E1. This area was at the time crime ridden and it is marked on a map, together with pictures.

On the night of her murder, 30 September 1888, she had been arrested earlier by PC Louis Robinson for drunkenness and was held in police custody in Bishopsgate police station until about 1.00 am. There was later criticism of her late release but there was a shortage of space. The museum has spy holes for visitors to look through, as if they were looking into the police cell with Kate inside it. They are at adult and child level and are very effective.

Her body was found at 1.44 am by PC Edward Watkins in Mitre Square, EC3. The museum has a map of the police beats. On the night of the murder Mitre Square was poorly lit and there were few residents. When PC Watkins walked through the square at 1.30 am he initially saw nothing unusual. When he found the body he alerted a nearby warehouse watchman and asked him to get help.

Although Kate was the fourth 'Jack the Ripper' victim, she was the only one to be murdered within the boundary of the City of London. Until then 'Jack the Ripper' investigations had been carried out by the Metropolitan Police. However, the City had increased police patrols in response and taken other preventive measures.

City Police Surgeon Dr Frederick Gordon Brown and Acting Commissioner Sir Henry Smith came straight to the scene. The murder investigation was led by Inspector James McWilliam, head of the City Detective Department.

Later that night the Metropolitan Police found part of a blood-stained apron and some graffiti on a wall. The graffiti was not proved to be connected. Photography was used by the City Police for the first time on this case, recording details of the crime scene.

Acting Commissioner Sir Henry Smith, who rushed to the murder scene by hansom cab, claimed he knew more about the Ripper murders than anyone else. He had issued orders that someone like Catherine Eddowes should be followed and men stationed to 'guard the approaches'. However, his orders were not followed and the murderer escaped.

Siege

Another section of the museum is dedicated to the Houndsditch Murders and the Siege of Sidney Street. On the evening of 16 December 1910 beat officer PC Piper heard suspicious noises coming from a building in Houndsditch and called for assistance. The noises came from an armed gang of Latvians, mainly revolutionaries and anarchists, trying to rob a jewellery shop. When police tried to stop them the gang fired, killing three officers: Sergeant Bentley, Sergeant Tucker and PC Choat, and wounding Sergeant Bryant and PC Woodhams.

A search for the gang ensued. The leader, George Gardstein, had been injured and was hiding in a house in Stepney. His doctor alerted police but by the time they arrived he had died. An award was offered for the others and on 2 January 1911 Fritz Svaars and William Sokolow were cornered in a house in Sidney Street, E1.

Thus began the armed Siege of Sidney Street. The cornered fugitives kept firing on the police and eventually Winston Churchill, the Home Secretary, ordered the Scots Guards in to help. The siege ended when the house caught fire and the gang members died in the blaze.

The gang had about fourteen members altogether, of which three were women. Some had connections to foreign anarchist or revolutionary organisations. Most were caught but some fled abroad. At the trial nearly all the gang were found not guilty due to a lack of evidence. The only one to be found guilty was Nina Vassileva and she later had her sentence overturned on a technicality.

Displayed are photographs and short biographies of the police officers involved. There are also pictures of the siege, a photograph of the 'wanted' posters and a memorial card to the police officers who died. It remains one of the biggest

Displays for the Houndsditch Murders trial.

incidences of police loss of life and injury in this country. The public sent in donations to their families and the widows of the sergeants received life pensions of thirty shillings a week. Afterwards there were parliamentary debates about immigration and how badly armed the police were.

An impressive wooden scale model of the house where the Houndsditch murders took place is exhibited. This was made by City of London Police to be used at the trial. Next to it is displayed a replica of a Mauser pistol, as used by the gang. In another display case are medals awarded to those involved, an Order of Service for the burial service at St Paul's Cathedral, a spring lock from one of the buildings the gang rented, a memorial plaque and some bullet fragments from Houndsditch and Sidney Street. There are also a cap, gas cylinder, knife, rubber tubing and a torch used by the gang.

Police Life

The museum also has a section on officer welfare. Police conditions in the Victorian era were poor. They were badly paid and men only stayed in the force for an average of four years. In 1865 a police hospital was founded at Bishopsgate by City of London Police Surgeon George Borlase Childs. Treatment was free and within a short time sickness in the City Police had gone down. The hospital was in use until the creation of the NHS.

Officers had to live in the City so that they could respond quickly to emergencies but there was a lack of suitable accommodation so housing conditions were often bad. Commissioner Daniel Whittle Harvey solved the problem by recommending building apartments for married officers and incorporating accommodation for single officers within police stations. On 26 May 1908 new apartments for married officers were opened at New Street, Bishopsgate. Displayed are some pictures of the interiors and exteriors.

There is also a section on ambulances. There were no ambulances before 1907, when there was a suggestion that horse-drawn ambulances could be introduced. The City of London Corporation decided to use two electric ambulances instead, driven by police officers. By 1927 they were replaced by petrol-driven vehicles. There were fifty-two call boxes around the city to summon an ambulance when necessary. In 1949 the service was taken over by the NHS. There is a picture of a 1910 motor ambulance. Displays in this area include a pedometer used until the 1940s and a portrait of George Borlase Childs.

War

The next area of the museum deals with the period of the First and Second World Wars.

London was bombed by Zeppelin airships between 1915 and 1918 and there were a lot of casualties, both police and civilian. Many police officers joined the army, but their numbers were made up by the First and Second Police Reserves. These were forces set up in 1912 by the Commissioner, the First from police pensioners and the Second from younger men. These forces would later become the City of London's Special Constabulary.

In 1914 the Defence of the Realm Act was brought into force restricting the movement of foreign nationals. One of the Police's duties was to register them. There is a reproduction of a poster directed to Alien Enemies telling them to remain at their registered place of residence from 9.00 pm to 5.00 am. There are also pictures of sand-bagged police stations.

After the First World War, police throughout the country, including the City of London, went on strike over pay. The Commissioner dismissed some of the strikers. A committee was set up and a pay rise allowed but the force was forbidden to be unionised.

The Second World War brought more destruction to the City during the bombing campaign known as the Blitz. In 1940 there were air raids for fifty-seven nights in a row. As in the First World War the reserves were drafted in to help out.

Constable Fred Tibbs and Constable Arthur Cross took photographs of the devastation caused by the air raids and there is a display of their photographs – you may recognise some of them. Their normal duties would have been far more routine, such as taking police identity photographs. The display case here includes an incendiary device from the Second World War.

There is a section on police sport. In 1886 the Police Athletics Club was set up offering many sports to participate in. The City of London Police won

Olympic medals for tug of war in 1908, 1912 and 1920. The 1920 medal is on display. The event was then dropped, which means the City of London Police are still the reigning Olympic champions. There is a large photograph of the tug of war team on the wall. In 1908 they also won medals for wrestling and boxing.

Post-war to the 1970s

The next area covers the period 1946-72. After the Second World War a third of the City had been destroyed and a lot of officers did not return to the force. Technology was advancing and the City of London Police underwent many changes. In 1966 Wood Street Police Station became the new headquarters.

The section on communication is particularly interesting. Originally communication was by word of mouth or the postal system; then a telegraphic system. The police had their own telephone line by the early 1900s. From the 1950s they had walkie-talkies and radios. There was also a database with details on vehicles and wanted persons. The police have always made use of technological innovations and are now moving into 4G digital technology. The display case includes a communication box board.

There is a blue call box on display. These were used until the 1980s. In 1907 fifty-two call boxes were installed in the City. The blue ones were introduced in 1965 and members of the public could use them to call the police. Mobile phones later rendered them obsolete. There is one on display in Guildhall Yard, against the east wall of St Lawrence Jewry but it is not usable.

Some police forces had been recruiting women since the 1920s, but the City Police only started when they were understaffed after the Second World War. One sergeant and six constables were recruited. Before that the police had used nursing matrons to look after female prisoners. During the Second World War women could join the Women's Auxiliary Police Corps to help with war work.

Twentieth century policing.

At first the women police officers did not work at night and they only worked with women and children, but by the mid-1970s they were involved in all police work and by the 1990s they were holding high rank. In 1995 Judy Davison became a Commander and she was the first female member of the Association of Chief Police Officers to come from the City of London Police. There is a picture of a Metropolitan Policewoman from 1931, and more modern photographs of City of London policewomen, showing how their role has developed.

After the Second World War there was a shortage of staff in the police. In 1951 Commissioner Colonel Sir Arthur Young established the Police Cadets to help solve the problem. Cadets would study for their O and A levels at the City College for Further Education and also learn about policing at the Training School. There was a strong emphasis on sport. They would then join the police when they reached 18. In 1973 female cadets were admitted. Today the cadets are for teenage volunteers who want to assist with crime prevention and the community in general.

Nearby is a display concerning the Moorgate tube train disaster of 1975. An underground train crashed at Moorgate station killing forty-three people and injuring seventy-four. The police had a Major Incident Plan which was put into action, including a vehicle that was loaded with all the equipment necessary to deal with the situation. There are pictures of the news headlines on the wall and a photograph of the commemoration plaque at Moorgate station.

Protest and Terrorism

There have been occasional changes to the City boundaries and many advances in technology and communications, especially since the Second World War. London is a major financial and tourist centre, bringing with it new associated threats. The City Police are now primarily involved with economic crime, terrorism and pubic order.

The last four decades have seen some high profile events, including major incidents and national celebrations. An early example of controlling public order was the anti-Catholic Gordon Riots of 1780, which was one of the causes of rethinking policing as the watchmen could not cope. More recent protests have included Stop the City, J18 and Occupy. The City Police have reacted to these with changes in riot uniforms and they often work in partnership with the Metropolitan Police.

This leads to a section on the Suffragettes. This was a campaigning movement in the early twentieth century to achieve votes for women. Some of their activities were violent. Two of their bombs from 1912 are displayed, and photographs of the police struggling with and arresting suffragettes, including their leader Emmeline Pankhurst.

Another modern section deals with counter-terrorism. The Irish Republican Army (IRA) were active from the 1970s to the 1990s killing and injuring many people, destroying buildings and causing millions of pounds worth of damage. Significant acts of terrorism included a car bomb outside the Old Bailey in 1973, another bomb in 1992 at St Mary Axe and another at Bishopsgate in 1993. There is a display of an officer's helmet damaged in the Old Bailey explosion. The officer survived.

One of the City Police responses was the 'Ring of Steel' in the early 1990s. A series of cameras and checkpoints were installed and entry was restricted to certain City streets. This developed into Automatic Number Plate Recognition (ANPR) where registration numbers are checked against a database.

Technology

Forensics is the use of scientific data to help solve crimes. The City of London Police has its own Forensics Services Team, with a fingerprint bureau, chemical enhancement laboratory, coroners' office and high-tech crime unit. This covers investigation of economic crime, identification of disaster victims and examination of crime scenes. They work with labs that offer DNA profiling and drugs and toxicological analysis. They are engaged in research to push back technological frontiers such as new methods of facial recognition.

CCTV helps identify criminals and facial recognition is very important. If there are no photos, crime witnesses are critical. In the 1970s they would use 'Photo-fit' kits to build up a face, using facial characteristics, or police artists would sometimes create a face on information given. Now they use 'E-Fit' (Electronic Facial Identification Technique). An interactive device to see if you could be a super-recogniser – someone who can recall most of the faces they see – tests the museum visitor.

There is also a section covering forgery, which has evolved over the years, with a glass case containing note and coin forgeries, the most recent from 1991. There are even fake gold bars.

The City of London is the centre of UK finance and the City of London Police specialises in fraud, as well as investigating financial crime nationwide. As technology advances, cybercrime has become a significant challenge. To tackle it the City Police keep up with technological developments and the threat technology can present, working with other interested parties on issues ranging from identity theft to money laundering.

The section on animals looks at how dogs can be used to search for firearms, explosives, drugs and cash. Horses were originally hired for ceremonies and for escort duty with the Lord Mayor. The police have had their own stables since 1947 and have nine horses at the moment. Today they are used for ceremonial events, to emphasise police presence and to control large crowds.

The last display area is a corridor with display cases on both sides. On the left is a selection of uniforms as they have changed over the decades, starting with the original constable's uniform from the 1840s, together with a tipstaff, handcuffs, a bullseye lamp and a nineteenth century truncheon.

We see an inspector's uniform from the 1850s with top hat, and an inspector's uniform from the 1870s – helmets replaced top hats in 1865 and have kept more or less the same shape ever since. Displayed is the uniform of Superintendent Foster who worked on the Ripper case and a probably fake postcard to him from Jack the Ripper.

There is a prototype of a new helmet that was never used, a hospital orderly uniform from the late nineteenth century, a helmet and gas mask from the Second World War, a constable's uniform from the 1930s, a policewoman's truncheon (in use until the 1990s), a woman constable's uniform post-1969, and police kits and a constables' uniform from the 1980s.

To the right is a collection of weapons the police have confiscated: a fearsome collection of mostly knives, clubs and knuckle dusters.

Jack the Ripper.

Jack the Ripper is one of the most famous murderers of all time. The first of the modern serial killers, he was active from August to November 1888 in the East End of London. His identity remains a mystery. Much has been written about him and there are several theories as to who he was but there has never been a definitive answer.

There are plenty of guided walks advertised which visit the murder locations, although London's East End is now very different to how it was when the Ripper was active. There are also many books and articles on the details of the Ripper Murders.

The basic facts are these:

All five of his victims were women and believed to be working as prostitutes.

Friday 31 August. The body of Mary Ann Nichols was discovered in Buck's Row (now Durward Street), Whitechapel, E1, her throat cut and her body mutilated.

Saturday 8 September. The Ripper struck again, killing Annie Chapman in Hanbury Street, Spitalfields, E1. Again her throat was cut and the body mutilated.

Sunday 30 September. Elizabeth Stride and Catherine Eddowes were murdered on the same night. Elizabeth Stride was found in Dutfield's Yard off Berner Street (now Henriques Street), Whitechapel, E1, but there were no mutilations, suggesting the Ripper had been interrupted during the murder. Catherine Eddowes' body was found in Mitre Square, EC3. Her throat had also been cut and her body severely mutilated. Her story is covered in the City of London Police Museum as she was found within the City boundary.

Friday 9 November. The fifth and final victim was Mary Jane Kelly. She was discovered dead in her lodgings in Miller's Court off Dorset Street, Spitalfields, E1. Her throat had been cut and the body very badly mutilated.

No other murder has been officially attributed to Jack the Ripper.

Chapter 15

Events and Ceremonials: Exterior

Cart Marking Ceremony

The Worshipful Company of Carmen are number seventy-seven in the Livery Company order of precedence. Once a year, usually in July, they take over Guildhall Yard for an annual cart marking ceremony.

Above and overleaf: Carts for Cart Marking.

Since the seventeenth century, the Master of the Carmen and the Keeper of Guildhall, otherwise known as the Lord Mayor, 'mark' a variety of vehicles with a numbered brass plate and the City's arms; thus providing them with a license to carry out carting services within the City of London.

In reality none of the vehicles licensed during the ceremony will ply for hire or work in the City. Horse-drawn milk carts, vintage taxis and buses and the occasional modern delivery truck are the types of vehicle that usually take part. The ceremony is a throwback to the days when the City regulated the licenses for what we would today refer to as the haulage industry.

The origins of the Carmen as an organised guild go back to 1277, although it would not be until 1517 that they formed the Fraternity of St Catherine the Virgin and Martyr of Carters. Catherine of Alexandria was adopted as the Carmen's patron saint as she was martyred on the wheel. As part of the deal, and in return for their recognition, the Guild also committed to 'cleanse, purge and keep the streets clean'.

In 1681 there were 420 carts, which increased to 600 in 1835. By 1900 there were 111 and when the tradition of plying for hire ended in 1965 there were only 18 carts left. The Worshipful Company is strong in numbers though, and includes over 460 Liverymen. Following the ceremony they gather for a lunch in the Great Hall to celebrate their continuity and raise money for charity.

The London Pearly Kings & Queens Society Costermongers Harvest Festival Parade Service

Pearly Kings and Queens developed during the late nineteenth century. They are a very 'London' institution, there is nothing like them anywhere else. The Harvest Festival has taken place at Guildhall every September since 2000.

Henry Croft (1862-1930) was a market sweeper in Somers Town, fresh out of the orphanage and ambitious to progress in life. It wasn't money that motivated him, but charity work and helping people. Surrounded by the market costermongers (sellers of fruit and vegetables) and their donkey barrows, what caught his eye most were the clothes they wore. The costermongers had developed their own recognisable way of dressing. Their corduroy trousers, jackets and long corduroy

Pearly Harvest Festival in Guildhall Yard (permission with thanks to Adrian Scarborough).

waistcoats were decorated with mother-of-pearl buttons. The button designs would denote status in the costermonger community, where the 'elder statesmen' would keep order and resolve disputes.

Henry Croft wanted to raise money for orphans, and he thought that if he found a way to stand out in the crowd it would also draw attention to his charity work. So he collected the lost mother-of-pearl buttons he found while sweeping in the market and then sewed the buttons onto his suit, thus creating the vibrant and unique uniform we associate with the Pearlies. His money raising was such a success it soon spread across London. Charity-raising Pearly families developed, with the heads of the family being called the Pearly King and Queen. Since the days of Henry Croft their uniform has never changed – thousands of pearl buttons still go into decorating every suit.

The annual Harvest Festival starts at Guildhall Yard, when the Lord Mayor or one of the Sheriffs provides the welcoming speech. A communal dance around a Maypole is the central event. Marching bands, City dignitaries, and Chelsea Pensioners all add to the celebrations. London Borough Mayors, the British Legion, HMS *President* Naval Reserves, Scouts and Guides all provide support and colour to this annual London 'knees-up'.

The Pearlies then transport the food, and even some of the dignitaries, in barrows pulled by donkeys to the traditional church of the London cockney, the Church of St Mary le Bow in Cheapside. Here the Harvest Festival Service takes place. At the end of the service the sound of Bow bells peals across the City.

Christ's Hospital School Procession

Every year, on or near to St Matthews Day (21 September), the ex-pupils of Christ's Hospital School process from the Church of St Andrew, Holborn, to Guildhall. The school was founded in 1552 when King Edward VI, with the help of the Lord Mayor, established a school on vacant land which had once been part of Christ Church, Newgate.

Established to provide 'a little learning for fatherless children and other poor men's children' the school is also known as the Bluecoat School on account of the Tudor-style blue coat, blue breeches and yellow socks worn by the pupils. In its oldest surviving register from 1563, 264 boys and 132 girls were being educated.

During the Great Plague of 1665 the school lost thirty-two pupils, and disaster struck again in 1666 when it was destroyed in the Great Fire of London. Luckily this time no pupils died. They were educated and billeted at a site in Hertfordshire until the school was rebuilt in 1705. Christopher Wren designed the new Christ Church, as well as the South Front of the new school building. In 1902 the school relocated permanently to Horsham, West Sussex.

The reason for the service, parade and lunch at Guildhall is simply to maintain tradition and Christ's Hospital's historic link to the City of London. Every Lord

Mayor is vice-president of the school and during the church service at St Andrew the school's Clerk of the Foundation hands a new list of School Governors to the Lord Mayor.

After the service some former pupils and present-day pupils in full Bluecoat uniform process to Guildhall with the school band and choir, where the Lord Mayor entertains the gathering to lunch, an event that is known as the Lord Mayor's 'largesse'.

> Former Christ's Hospital pupils include the Romantic poet Samuel Taylor Coleridge, architect Augustus Pugin, inventor of the bouncing bomb Barnes Wallis, and punk poet John Baine who is better known as Attila the Stockbroker.

Inter-Livery Pancake Race

Not all traditions are old. In 2004 the Worshipful Company of Poulters had the idea to run a pancake race for charity every Shrove Tuesday. This developed into the Inter-Livery Pancake Race and it's definitely not restricted to the Poulters. The races are run in Guildhall Yard and other Livery Companies taking part all make a contribution to the making of the pancakes or the running of the event.

The Poulters bring the eggs. The Fruiterers bring some lemons, the Cutlers the (plastic) forks and the Musicians provide musical entertainment. Full uniform Liveries are worn, although fancy dress is encouraged. Teams from Mansion House, the Old Bailey and Guildhall are also invited to compete. The Gunmakers start the races, with a loud bang, the Clockmakers time the heats and the Glovers supply the white gloves which must be worn by the competitors. The winning team is presented with a commemorative frying pan, supplied by the Ironmongers.

Perhaps in three or four hundred years they will still be competing for a frying pan every Shrove Tuesday and looking back at the venerable traditions of the Inter-Livery Pancake Race.

Chapter 16

Guildhall's Lost Buildings

Fire damage, bomb damage, rebuilding, reorganization and relocation: these are just some of the reasons why buildings that used to be part of Guildhall are no longer there. Apart from the Great Hall every building within Guildhall is not on its original site, or has completely disappeared. The old Library building survives but has made way for the new Library in the West Wing. The Art Gallery was bombed and rebuilt, yet its original building had earlier uses.

This chapter is concerned with the buildings sometimes mentioned, perhaps glimpsed on old plans or engravings, but no longer with us.

The Chapel and College of St Mary and St Mary Magdalene

A chapel and college of priests had been mentioned as early as the late thirteenth century, preceding the building of John Croxtone's Great Hall. The Bishop of Winchester supplied timbers for its completion in 1326 and by 1368 a custos (keeper) and five chaplains had been installed.

It served both as a chantry (where mass was chanted for the souls of wealthy benefactors) and a place of prayer for the Corporation when meeting for business at Guildhall. It may also have had links to the Society of Puy, a fraternity frequented by wealthy merchants for poetry and music competitions, often dedicated to the Virgin Mary.

Unfortunately, by 1417 the chaplains were deemed not to be up to their tasks and negligent in their duties. The Corporation seized the land and planned for the future. In 1429 King Henry VI granted letters patent to rebuild, and a much larger chapel was completed by 1446. Archaeological digs have discovered foundation stones with two names engraved on them. Both Henry Frowyk and Thomas Knollys were Lord Mayors, probable funders of the rebuilt chapel and, according to the engravings, they should be 'known to God'.

This new chapel, like the old, was situated on the south-east side of the Great Hall, almost abutting its southern wall. The chaplains relocated to new living quarters to the north side of the Great Hall, although they, and others, continued to be interred in the chapel.

The Chapel, 1820.

Some things however never changed and during the 1540s Bishop of London Edmund Bonner was obliged to bring order to the unruly and lazy priests. They were forbidden to enter taverns or wear weapons (within the chapel) and were fined for slander and fighting. The Reformation dealt a final blow and in 1548 the chapel was suppressed and acquired by King Edward VI. The three remaining chaplains were pensioned off.

The Corporation purchased the chapel building from the Crown in 1550 and continued to use it as a place of prayer for Lord Mayor's services and for Corporation meetings and entertainments. It did undergo some slight changes when in 1643 the stained-glass windows were destroyed on the order of local Protestant priests, for being 'monuments of idolatry and superstition'. People also continued to be buried here – as late as 1705 William Man, aged 76 and previously Swordbearer to the Lord Mayor, was interred within the chapel.

The Great Fire of 1666 damaged but did not destroy the chapel and by the late 1600s it was described as 'a pleasant large Chapel of the Gothic order except for the upper windows which were burnt in the Great Fire and rebuilt in the Tuscan style'. Despite its understated grandeur a narrow passage known as 'Cut Throat Alley' separated the chapel from the Great Hall.

By 1782 the chapel had been superseded by St Lawrence Jewry as the main chapel of the Lord Mayor and Corporation and it became incorporated into the various court buildings that functioned around Guildhall. Its demolition in 1820 was not universally popular – some had favoured restoration. The chapel's many monuments were moved to St Lawrence Jewry following demolition.

By 1822 new Courts, designed by William Mountague, had been built, and with the closure of these courts in the 1880s the buildings were again re-purposed, this time to become part of the new Art Gallery. This building was in turn almost destroyed during the Second World War and has now been replaced by the extended Yard to the east and the new Art Gallery.

Blackwell Hall

In 1293 John de Banquelle, Alderman of Dowgate Ward, purchased some land slightly to the south-east of the old Guildhall, from Sir Roger de Clifford, a nobleman connected to the royal court. Records state that in 1337 timbers from Guildhall were stored in the gardens abutting the garden of John de Bankwell; timbers which were later used for the repair of Cripplegate.

Around 1395 the Corporation purchased the land, which by now contained buildings, for £50, either from the de Bankwell family or, as seems more likely, from King Richard II who had somehow taken possession. In 1397, during Richard Whittington's first mayoralty, the buildings were turned into a cloth fair,

Blackwell Hall, 1811.

at first the only cloth fair in the City, where 'strangers and foreigners' could trade in wool and cloth.

'Foreigners' in this context referred to traders who were not City Freemen or members of the Drapers Company. 'Foreigners and strangers' had a reputation for undercutting Freemen and avoiding customs and duties due to the Crown. The hours they could trade at Blackwell Hall were severely restricted.

Blackwell Hall was just to the south of the chapel on the east side of Guildhall Yard. Its name was clearly derived from the de Bankwells and it soon became a main trading cloth exchange. John Stow, at the end of the sixteenth century, describes it as 'long since employed as a weekly market place for all sorts of woollen cloths broad and narrow, brought from all parts of this realm, there to be sold'. A complete rebuild took place in 1588, which was unfortunate, because Blackwell Hall was completely destroyed during the Great Fire in 1666.

By 1672 a rebuilt Blackwell Hall was completed and divided into separate trading halls: Devonshire, Gloucestershire, Worcestershire, Kentish, Medley, Spanish and Blanket. A system also developed whereby 'factors' were able to borrow large amounts on credit, enabling them to dominate the trade between merchants and clients.

By the end of the eighteenth-century, business was in decline. Even the factors could not compete with the mechanised cloth trade of the north of England, who dealt directly with their own clients.

In 1820 Blackwell Hall was demolished, and like the Chapel it was replaced by a new building which became the Bankruptcy Court. In 1886 it became part of the Art Gallery, surviving until it was seriously damaged by bombs in the Second World War. The new Art Gallery also sits on the site of the old Blackwell Hall.

Guildhall School of Music and Drama

This world-famous university of the arts was founded in 1880. Originally called the Guildhall Orchestral Society, it was governed by the Music Committee of the Corporation of the City of London.

The first intake of sixty-two part time students originally studied in an old warehouse at the north-west end of Guildhall, facing Aldermansbury. Conditions were far from perfect, as we read that 'the gentleman who taught the drums gave his lessons in the coal cellar'.

Success was swift and with 2,500 students by 1886 the school relocated to a new building in John Carpenter Street near Victoria Embankment. This was one of Sir Horace Jones's last buildings and was purpose-built for the school. Accommodating forty-five studios, each wall was constructed of concrete one foot thick. It survives today as offices on the corner with Tallis Street. The decorated stone panel above the entrance is still inscribed with the words 'Guildhall School of Music'.

In 1934 the name was officially extended to Guildhall School of Music and Drama and in 1977 the school returned to its present site near to Guildhall, within the Barbican development on Silk Street, EC2. It is still funded and administered by the Corporation.

Today there are 800 students. Alumni include James Galway, Max Jaffa, George Martin, Jacqueline du Pré, Bryn Terfel, Daniel Craig, Peter Cushing, Damian Lewis, Ewan McGregor and Alfred Molina.

Gresham College

The street on which Guildhall stands is called Gresham Street, named after Gresham College which used to stand next to the Guildhall site. The will of Sir Thomas Gresham, founder of the Royal Exchange, established Gresham College in 1597. The college originally based itself in Gresham's mansion near Bishopsgate, where Tower 42 now stands.

Although the college doesn't award degrees it is regarded as the oldest university in England after Oxford and Cambridge. Its lecturers and its students are all part time.

In 1657 a 25-year-old Christopher Wren became its Professor of Astronomy, providing free lectures for three years. The Royal Society established itself here in 1660, with Wren also becoming a founder member. In 1710 the college relocated to another site near Fetter Lane and it wasn't until 1842 that New Gresham College established itself next to Guildhall on the corner of Basinghall Street.

By this time Gresham College had gained the nickname 'Wiseacre Hall'. A wiseacre, according to the Dictionary of the Vulgar Tongue, was a 'foolish, conceited fellow'. In 1881 Gresham Street was created by widening the narrow thoroughfares, from the west, of St Anne's Lane, Maiden Lane, Lad Lane and Cateaton Street.

In 1991 the college moved to its present home in Barnard's Inn Hall near Holborn. The original professorships of Astronomy, Divinity, Geometry, Law, Music, Physic and Rhetoric have expanded to include Commerce, Environment and Information Technology. There are 140 free lectures every year and the Lord Mayor is still President of the College.

Commission of Sewers

The Commission of Sewers occupied a large office in the north side of the Guildhall offices, approximately where North Wing is today. The 1531 Act of Sewers obliged local authorities to take permanent responsibility for land drainage and flood prevention, not as we would think today for the dispersion of household waste.

The City of London eventually developed its own Commission of Sewers in 1669 (slightly post-dating the Great Fire, which seems too much of a coincidence). Subsequent Acts of Parliament extended the functions of all such Commissions to include construction of sewers and drains, cleaning and paving.

The 1848 Metropolitan Commission of Sewers Act excluded the City, and the Commission of Sewers at Guildhall continued to operate independently. The main purpose of the 1848 Act was to enforce regulations ridding London of its 200,000 cesspits. All household drains were henceforth to connect to sewers which led directly to the River Thames. This plan, which turned the Thames into the main conduit of London's human waste, led directly to the Great Stink of 1858.

The City of London Sewers Act 1897 dissolved the Commission, handing responsibility over to Common Council until 1947 when it merged with the Town Clerk's Office. Subsequent nationalisation and privatisation of Water Boards and Water Companies have taken responsibility away from local government.

Coopers' Hall

The Worshipful Company of Coopers is number thirty-six in the Livery Company rankings. It can trace its origins back 800 years and is first mentioned in public records in 1298.

The Guild's Charter of Incorporation is dated 1501 when certain powers were granted to the Coopers. It was tasked with viewing and gauging all vessels (barrels and casks) used for the storage of ale, beer and soap and branding those inspected.

The expansion of England's navy from the sixteenth century increased the work and wealth of the company. All goods for storage such as food, drink, ammunition and cargo would have been held in barrels and casks.

In 1522 the Guild warden, John Baker, left the company his house next to Guildhall in Basinghall Street, which became their Livery Hall. Although it went through various improvements and changes through the centuries, for instance after the Great Fire of 1666, the Hall stood continuously at the north-east edge of the Guildhall site. On 29 December 1940 it was completely destroyed by enemy action and never rebuilt. The land was sold to the Corporation and in 1958 the company moved to its present home, a seventeenth century merchant's house in Devonshire Square, EC3.

The Courts

The Court system today is the result of over 1000 years of expansion, reorganisation and, more recently, simplification. Although the courts tended to be based in Westminster, there were smaller courts in the City, often housed in buildings that were part of the Guildhall site. These were mainly civil courts dealing with property disputes, debt and personal injury and were separate to the Great Trials once held in the Great Hall. They included:

Court of the Wardmote, Court of Request (later called the Court of Conscience), Court of Common Pleas, Mayor's Court, Court of Exchequer (also known as the

Left: The Chapel
used as the Court of
Request, 1815.

Below: The Mayor's
Court, Guildhall
Buildings.

Court of the King's Bench), Court of the Queen's Bench, Sheriff's Court, Court of Bankruptcy and the Court of Justice.

The only Court now based at Guildhall, in Guildhall Buildings, is the combined Mayor's Court and City of London Court. It's the only County Court in the United Kingdom without the word 'County' in its name.

The Mayor's Court hears civil cases specific to the City jurisdiction concerning contract law (legal disagreements), tort (personal suffering or injury) and ejectment (land disputes). The City of London Court (known as the Sheriff's Court until 1852) tends to hear claims dealing more with money or property, sometimes known as 'replevin' from Old French 'to recover' or 'redeem'.

Clockmakers' Museum

The Clockmakers' Company was established by Royal Charter in 1631 and is number sixty one in the livery companies order of precedence. It is the oldest surviving horological institution in the world.

The Company Library was founded in 1813 and in 1925 it moved into the Guildhall Library, where it still forms part of the collection.

The Clockworkers' Collection (later Museum) started in 1814. It is the worlds oldest collection of clocks and watches, with exhibits dating from c.1600. In 1874 the museum moved to Guildhall and in 2015 relocated to the Science Museum, London SW7, where it is free to view in the public galleries.

St Lawrence and St Mary Magdalene Drinking Fountain

The drinking fountain was erected in 1866 by two local parish churches, St Lawrence Jewry and St Mary Magdalene. It originally stood to the north of the church of St Lawrence Jewry but was dismantled in 1970 to make way for Richard Gilbert Scott's new West Wing.

Architect John Robinson designed the elaborate 32 x 9 foot Gothic Revivalist structure. The lower half was constructed of Portland stone and the upper in polished granite.

Joseph Durham added three sculptures. In stone is St Lawrence holding the gridiron symbol of his martyrdom and St Mary Magdalene holding a cross. A bronze relief features Moses striking the rock at Horeb for water, an Israelite mother and child at his feet. It was from here the drinking water flowed through an outlet into a rounded dish.

Cholera and other water-borne diseases were still rife during this period and providing access to fresh, uncontaminated water became a common act of philanthropy. From the 1850s most public drinking fountains were provided by the Metropolitan Free Dinking Association, which makes this parish church donation more unusual.

Following its dismantlement into 150 pieces the fountain had a nomadic existence, allegedly ending up in a pig farm in Essex. In 2009 it was reassembled and restored in preparation for its new location, which in 2010 was Carter Lane Gardens on the south side of St Paul's Cathedral, where it can be seen today.

The Wren church of St Mary Magdalene was demolished in 1887 and stood close to where Knightrider Street is today.

Above: Guildhall Yard in the early twentieth century. The Drinking Fountain can be seen to the left.

Left: The Drinking Fountain in Carter Lane Gardens.

Chapter 17

Guildhall Today

The City of London Corporation is one of thirty-three London local authorities. Thirty-two others, including the City of Westminster and the Royal Borough of Kensington & Chelsea, make up Greater London.

The City of London is different to other boroughs though, being the historic centre of London and the main financial district. The Square Mile, actually 1.12 square miles, is the smallest by far of all London authorities. The Corporation head office is at Guildhall, as it has been for hundreds of years.

Greater London has almost nine million inhabitants. Those living in the Square Mile number only about eight thousand. Commercial properties and office blocks dominate the landscape. But because of its position as one of London's commercial hubs, and being the world's largest financial district, over 450,000 people commute to work in the City every working day. Ten million tourists visit the Square Mile and its attractions every year.

Guildhall functions mainly as any town hall would, responsible for local public services such as planning, registering births, marriages and deaths, street cleaning, children and family services, highways maintenance, adult social care, food services and environmental health, libraries, entertainment licences, street trading and adult learning.

But because of its unusual position, the Corporation's role historically expanded to support and promote London as the world's leading financial and business centre. It is also the fourth largest patron of arts in the UK, being involved in the Barbican Centre, Guildhall Art Gallery, Museum of London and the Guildhall School of Music & Drama.

Grants and social investments of up to £20 million are made every year through the City Bridge Trust to London community groups and charities, helping to increase skills and employment opportunities. The City Bridge Trust is the funding arm of the Bridge House Estates which owns Tower Bridge, London Bridge, Southwark Bridge and Blackfriars Bridge.

The Square Mile contains 200 open spaces and gardens; the Corporation is responsible for the upkeep of over 150 of them, as well as monuments and statues. The City also owns and maintains Hampstead Heath, Highgate Woods, Epping Forest, Queen's Park, West Ham Park and Ashtead Common. Four ancient markets are regulated by the City: Smithfield for dead meat, New Spitalfields for fresh produce, Billingsgate for fish, and Leadenhall, which has been converted into a shopping and eating area. The Central Criminal Court in Old Bailey is also maintained by the City.

The Chamberlain of London

The Chamberlain is based in Guildhall and is an official whose earliest references go back to 1237. The Chamberlain plays a part in some of the City's ceremonies, such as the swearing in of a new Lord Mayor and Sheriffs and they are themselves a High Officer of the Court of Aldermen.

Although regarded as a local government officer, whose main role is the Corporation's Director of Finance, there is one other function of the Chamberlain's office that is unlike any other. The Chamberlain's Court, overseen by the Clerk of the Chamberlain's Court, is a specific part of the department which administers the Freedom of the City of London.

'Freedom' has over time had various meanings. It generally referred to men that had served apprenticeships in the City and who were now free to join a guild and to trade independently. Originally only the sons of Freemen could serve apprenticeships and enter the guilds, a privilege passed down through the generations.

Chamberlain's Court 1787-1882.

In the days when many people were serfs, freemen were neither serfs nor indentured to work for a landowner or noble. If born a serf, freedom could be purchased, and although it didn't guarantee wealth, freedom ensured the right to earn one's own money and the benefits of certain human rights.

Freedom could also be gained if a serf ran away to a chartered town or city for one year and a day. Being granted Freedom of the City of London is really being given citizenship of the City.

Apprentices would once have become Freemen through 'Servitude', the seven-year training process all would have served. Some people can still gain freedom through 'Patrimony' if their fathers were Freemen before they were born. Most people nowadays gain freedom by 'Redemption'; freedom is purchased. Almost all Freemen are Liverymen or are nominated by two Liverymen, Aldermen or Common Councillors.

> Honorary Freedom is occasionally granted and is considered an honour. Many royals have been given Honorary Freedom. Some Prime Ministers have been honoured, for example Winston Churchill, and philanthropists such as Florence Nightingale. Military heroes, for instance Viscount Montgomery of Alamein, are often honoured, and sometimes foreigners, such as Nelson Mandela.

Guildhall Library

'A free library, open to anyone without formality'

Guildhall Library today has the largest collection of books in the world dedicated to one city: London. Situated in the West Wing, with its main door in Aldermansbury, Guildhall Library is a free-to-use, reference-only library. The main floor of the library is made up of the Guildhall Library and City Business Library. The City of London Police Museum is accessible through the same entrance.

The library holds 200,000 titles representing over 500,000 volumes. Only five per cent of the library's collection is on display at any one time. Two climate controlled sub-basements preserve the oldest and most valuable parts of the collection.

The library holds a small collection of thirteen to the fifteenth century handwritten manuscript books. From the late fifteenth century onwards, books are printed, and this makes up most of the library collection.

As well as books, the library collection includes thousands of pamphlets and broadsheets. Pamphlets are small, unbound publications numbering at most a few pages and date from the sixteenth century onwards. They would cover any topic from political, to news to promotional. Broadsheets tend to be dated from the seventeenth and eighteenth century. They are single-sided printed sheets that were mostly pasted onto walls. Like pamphlets they covered all subjects but were also used as advertisements and promo sheets.

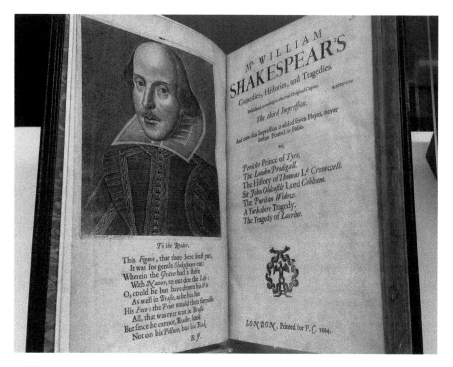

William Shakespeare, *Third Folio*. Permission of Guildhall Library.

The City Business Library evolved out of the Business Reference Room in the old library. It even moved into its own premises on London Wall but rejoined the main library in the West Wing in the early twenty-first century.

The Guildhall Library collection holds far too many titles to list here, but does include:

William Shakespeare: First Folio (1623), Third Folio (1664) and Fourth Folio (1685).

Chronicles of France: An illuminated late-fourteenth-century manuscript book of the history of France. The text is in French, although the illustrations are by a Flemish artist.

Peter Di Riga Bible: A thirteenth century manuscript bible which was part of the library's original collection, until taken away by the Duke of Somerset in 1549. Guildhall Library reacquired the bible during the 1920s, quite legally.

Bills of Mortality: This printed book is a statistical record of burials and causes of death in London from the sixteenth to the nineteenth century. It includes the Great Plague of 1665.

Chained Bible: A late-sixteenth century printed bible, with chain intact (to avoid theft). Although it is owned by the Worshipful Company of Tylers and Bricklayers the Guildhall Library looks after it.

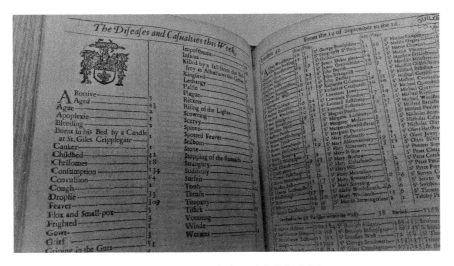

Bills of Mortality, Great Plague 1665. Permission of Guildhall Library.

Clockmakers Library and the Antiquarian Horological Society Collection: The world's largest collection of books on clocks and watches. During the seventeenth and eighteenth centuries, London was the biggest centre of clock making in the world.

Elizabeth David (1913-92): Her personal library of over 900 books. Elizabeth David was a British cookery writer who influenced the revival and interest in home cooking.

The archives of eighty Livery Companies, of the London Stock Exchange and of Lloyd's Marine Collection.

Guildhall Art Gallery

The Art Gallery today has a permanent collection of approximately 4,000 works of art and displays around 123 in the galleries at any one time. Works not on permanent display can appear in exhibitions within the gallery and be loaned for exhibitions abroad. With so much kept in the archive the gallery re-hangs and rotates works on a continuous basis.

Still included within the collection are those works owned by the City of London Corporation. Some are displayed offsite, for instance in Mansion House, the official residence of the Lord Mayor. The Gallery is funded by the City of London Corporation. Some exhibitions are part-funded by the Heritage Lottery Fund or other external partnership funds.

The Art Gallery is still free, still open on Sundays as well as weekdays, and expects around 100,000 visitors to see its collections, exhibitions and the amphitheatre every year.

Chapter 18

Visiting Guildhall

There are eight areas within Guildhall which are all publicly accessible and free of charge:

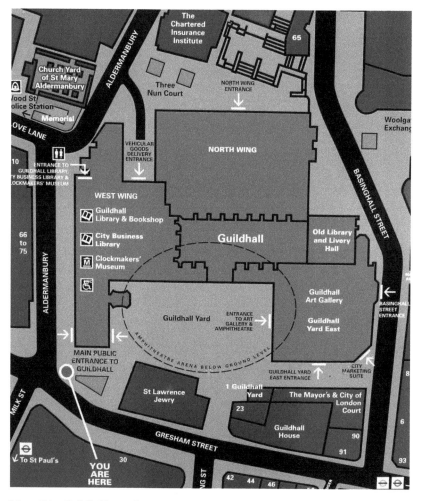

Map of the Guildhall complex.

1. Guildhall Art Gallery

The mission of the Art Gallery has always been to display 'a Collection of Art Treasures worthy of the capital city'. The gallery has on display art works from its permanent collection of paintings, drawings and sculptures. Two collections are rated as being of international importance: the Victorian art collection, which includes works by many of the Pre-Raphaelite Brotherhood such as Millais and Holman Hunt, and the historical paintings of London. The London collection includes seventeenth century engravings to contemporary paintings and photography, and artists from Canaletto to Leighton.

The Art Gallery has temporary exhibitions running throughout the year and a book shop.

Open: Monday to Saturday 10am - 5pm, Sunday 12 noon - 4pm. Free Entry.
Free Tours: Tuesday, Friday, Saturday at 12.15, 1.15, 2.15, 3.15.
www.cityoflondon.gov.uk/guildhallartgallery

2. Roman Amphitheatre and Guildhall Yard

The Amphitheatre is situated in the basement level of the Art Gallery. Now designated an ancient monument it was once the centre of entertainment in Roman Londinium. It was large enough to seat an audience of 7,000, who would watch fighting animals, executions and gladiatorial combat. Today we can see parts of the wall, east gate, entrance tunnel and drains.

A modern light exhibition surrounds the visitor, illustrating the scale of the old amphitheatre. Guildhall Yard has an elliptical display of black tiles set into the paving which shows the size of the amphitheatre to the observer above ground.

Open: Monday to Saturday 10am - 5pm, Sunday 12 noon - 4pm. Free Entry.
www.cityoflondon.gov.uk/amphitheatre

Roman
Amphitheatre.

167

3. City of London Heritage Gallery

The Heritage Gallery is a small space within the Art Gallery showcasing documents and artefacts from the City archives and archaeological digs. Displays are regularly rotated and the documents changed. Recently on display have been King John's charter of 1215 granting the City the right to appoint a Lord Mayor; the Shakespeare Deed, carrying Shakespeare's signature; and the William charter of 1067 when William the Conqueror recognized the ancient privileges of the City.

Open: Monday to Saturday 10am - 5pm, Sunday 12 noon - 4pm. Free Entry.
www.cityoflondon.gov.uk/heritagegallery

4. The Guildhall Library

Although it began as a religious library in 1425 the modern Guildhall Library was established in 1828. Guildhall Library has become the largest library devoted to London history, ceremony, architecture, buildings, trades, people and London life

Guildhall Library Exhibition. Permission of Guildhall Library.

in general. Its archive of books, manuscripts, pamphlets, brochures and posters is the world's largest collection of printed material concerned with one single city.

The Guildhall Library and City Business Library are used mainly for research and reference and are open to the public free of charge. Talks, book launches, exhibitions and evening events take place through the year. The City Business Library also specializes in new business start-up workshops.

Open: Monday to Friday 9.30am – 5pm (Wednesday 7.30pm). Alternate Saturdays 10am - 5pm.
www.cityoflondon.gov.uk/guildhalllibrary

5. City of London Police Museum

The City of London Police Museum relocated to Guildhall in 2016 and is accessible through the Guildhall Library entrance. The City of London Police patrol only the square mile of the City of London and were established in 1839, ten years after the Metropolitan Police.

The Museum tells the history of this small police force and the criminal stories it has been involved in for almost 200 years. These range from dealing with a Jack the Ripper murder, Suffragette protests, Jewish anarchists and IRA terrorists.

It wasn't all crime fighting. City of London police officers also won gold medals in the 1908 London Olympics. Displays, equipment, photographs, audio visuals and uniforms relate the fascinating tales and often dangerous work of the City Police.

Open: Monday to Friday 9.30am - 5pm (Wednesday 7.30pm). Saturday 10am - 4pm. Free Entry.
www.cityoflondon.gov.uk/policemuseum

6. Guildhall Great Hall

The ancient centrepiece of Guildhall and its oldest building, the Great Hall is a medieval Gothic building without compare in the City. Built in the early fifteenth century the Great Hall survived the Great Fire and the Blitz and is still the ceremonial heart of the City of London Corporation. It has the second largest single span timber roof in England after Westminster Hall.

From Coronation banquets to Lord Mayor's banquets the Great Hall has been the setting for great ceremony, but also great trials. Lady Jane Grey was amongst the many who were tried here before meeting their end at Tower Hill.

The Great Hall is home to memorial statues of British heroes the City has chosen to honour. John Bacon's *Duke of Wellington* and Oscar Nemon's *Winston Churchill* sit either side of *Horatio Nelson*. All look across towards the two Guildhall Giants that are Gog and Magog, mythical guardians of the City of London.

Open: Monday to Saturday 10am - 4.30pm. Sunday 10am - 4.30pm (May to September). Access is subject to availability and pre-booking, closure may take place at short notice for functions and events. Phone to check in advance: 020 7332 3646.

Tours are provided by City of London tour guides. Details available at: www.cityoflondonguides.com/tours/guildhall-monthly-tours

7. The Church of St Lawrence Jewry

A City church with origins going back over 800 years. St Lawrence Jewry is now the official Church of the City of London Corporation. The medieval church burnt down during the Great Fire in 1666 and was one of the grandest of the fifty-one City churches redesigned and rebuilt by Sir Christopher Wren.

Bombing in 1940 destroyed much of the church and again it was rebuilt, largely to Wren's original plans. Beautifully decorated once more in the Baroque style, it has some of the finest stained-glass windows found in City churches.

Open: Monday - Friday 8am - 5pm. Free Entry.
There are often music recitals, and coffee and refreshments are available in the vestibule.
www.stlawrencejewry.org.uk

8. The City Centre

The City Centre is accessible from the corner of Guildhall Buildings and Basinghall Street. This is the place to explore the history of the City's architecture and building heritage.

The City Centre is home to the City of London's official architectural model of the Square Mile. To a scale of 1:500 it provides a panoramic and birds-eye view of the City in a model that could itself be art. Wood and laser cutting and 3D printing are used to make every structure, street and alley, as well as those buildings as yet unbuilt but with planning permission. This is a fascinating glimpse into what the City will look like in the future.

Opening times:
Model Exhibition: Friday & Saturday 10am - 5pm.
Gallery: Monday to Friday 10am - 5pm.
Free Entry.
www.thecitycentre.london

The City Centre model. Permission of City Centre.

City of London Coat of Arms.

Bibliography and Sources

Ackroyd, Peter, *London: the Biography*, 2000

Ackroyd, Peter, *Tudors (The History of England)*, 2012

Architect, The, The Guildhall Library and Museum, 9 November 1872

Architect, The, The New Guildhall, November 1974

Architect & Building News, The, Guildhall Scheme, 28 December 1966

Architect & Contract Reporter, The, The Guildhall Library, 28 July 1893

Architects Journal, Ridley Declares Guildhall an Arena, 13 July 1988

Arnold, Caroline, *Sheep Over London Bridge - The Freedom of the City of London*, 1995

Baddeley, Sir John James, *The Guildhall of the City of London*, 1939, 7th edition

Barron, Caroline, *The Medieval Guildhall of London*, 1974

Bateman, Nick, *Gladiators at the Guildhall*, 2000

Bateman, Nick, *Roman London's Amphitheatre*, 2011

Bellany, Alastair, *Oxford Dictionary of National Biography*, Sir Gervase Helwys, 2016

Birchall, Heather, *Pre-Raphaelites*, 2016

Bowsher, David, Dyson, Tony, Holder, Nick and Howell, Isca, *The London Guildhall*, 2007

Bradley, Simon & Pevsner, Nikolaus, *The Buildings of England, London 1: The City of London*, 2002

Brigden, Susan, *Oxford Dictionary of National Biography*, Henry Howard, 2016

Bronkhurst, Judith, *Oxford Dictionary of National Biography*, William Holman Hunt, 2016

Builder, The, Guildhall Improvement Scheme, 20 January 1939

Builder, The, Reconstruction of the Roof and Restoration of Guildhall, 15 November 1954

Building, Guildhall West Crypt, 23 February 1973

Building, Guildhall Precinct Reconstructed, 31 January 1975

Building, On Site: Guildhall Yard, 8 September 1995

Building Design, Unearthing Past Glories, 25 August 1995

Bullen, J.B., *Oxford Dictionary of National Biography*, Dante Gabriel Rossetti, 2016

Burton, Neil, The Guildhall and Guildhall Yard, 1988, unpublished notes

BIBLIOGRAPHY AND SOURCES

City of London Police Museum

Clayton, Anthony, *London's Coffee Houses*, 2003

Clifford, Alan, *John Tillotson*, Cross Way, 1986

Country Life, London's Modern Goth, 21 November 2002

De la Bédoyère, Guy, *Roman Britain, A New History*, 2013

Dobinson, Tee (Editor), *Treasures of the Guildhall Art Gallery*, 2016

Downes, Kerry, *Oxford Dictionary of National Biography*, Sir Christopher Wren, 2016

Encyclopaedia Judaica, 1973, 2nd Printing

Esterly, David, *Oxford Dictionary of National Biography*, Grinling Gibbons, 2016

Fairholt, F.W., *Gog and Magog*, 1859, The Book Tree reprint 2000

Foster-Brown, Rear Admiral R.S., '*Introduction to the Worshipful Company of Armourers and Brasiers*' 1964

Guildhall Art Gallery

Guildhall Roman Amphitheatre

Hartley, Carol, *Oxford Dictionary of National Biography*, Sir Thomas Bloodworth, 2016

Harwood, Elain, Guildhall Library, Guildhall Yard, City of London, 2003, unpublished notes

Hall, James, *Hall's Dictionary of Subjects and Symbols in Art*, 1996

Hope, Valerie, *My Lord Mayor*, 1989

Jagger, Paul D., *London Freeman's Guide*, Lord Mayor's Edition, 2016

Jeffery, Sally, The Old Library, Guildhall, 1998, unpublished notes

Keene, Derek, *Oxford Dictionary of National Biography*, Henry FitzAilwyn, 2016

Kenyon, Nicholas (Editor), *The City of London - A Companion Guide*, 2012

Knight, Vivien, *The History of the Guildhall Art Gallery*, 1999

Lambourne, Lionel, *Victorian Painting*, 1999

Lehmberg, Stanford, *Oxford Dictionary of National Biography*, Nicholas Throckmorton, 2016

Lock, Julian, *Oxford Dictionary of National Biography*, John Felton, 2016

Mansion House Plateroom

Marsh, Jan, *The Pre-Raphaelite Circle*, 2013

Matheuo, Demitrious, 'New Guildhall Gallery Opens', *Architects Journal*, 16 September 1999

MacCulloch Diarmaid, *Oxford Dictionary of National Biography*, Thomas Cranmer, 2016

McCoog, Thomas M, *Oxford Dictionary of National Biography*, Henry Garnett, 2016

Meyer, G.J., *The Tudors*, 2015

Newall, Christopher, *Oxford Dictionary of National Biography*, Frederic Leighton, 2016

Nightingale, Pamela, *Oxford Dictionary of National Biography*, Sir William Walworth, 2016

Parrott, Canon David, *The Windows of St Lawrence Jewry*, 2012

Parrott, Canon David, *St Lawrence Jewry*, 2014

Plowden, Alison, *Oxford Dictionary of National Biography, Lady Jane Grey*, 2016

Price, John Edward, *A Descriptive Account of the Guildhall of the City of London*, 1886

Richardson, H.A., 'Guildhall: English Oak in the Great Hall', *Wood*, April 1955

Rumbelow, Donald, *The Complete Jack the Ripper*, 1987

Rumbelow, Donald, *The Houndsditch Murders and the Seige of Sidney Street*, 1988

Samuel, Edgar, *Oxford Dictionary of National Biography*, Dr Rodrigo Lopez, 2016

Spence, Keith, '550 Years of the Guildhall Library', *Country Life*, 14 November 1974

Stephens, F.G., *Dante Gabriel Rossetti*, 1894, Leopold Classic Library reprint

Stroud, Dorothy, *George Dance, Architect 1741-1825*, 1971

Studdard, John, *Whittington to World Financial Centre - The City of London and its Lord Mayor*, 2008

Sutton Anne F, *Oxford Dictionary of National Biography*, Richard Whittington, 2016

Thomas, Peter D.G., *Oxford Dictionary of National Biography*, John Wilkes, 2016

Thurley, Simon, 'The Medieval Guildhall', Melhuish Lecture, March 2017

Tucker, Tony, *City of London Churches*, 2013

Turner, Christopher, *London Churches Step by Step*, 1987

Ward-Jackson, Philip, *Public Sculpture of the City of London*, 2003

Warner, Malcolm, *Oxford Dictionary of National Biography*, Sir John Everett Millais, 2016

Watt, Diane, *Oxford Dictionary of National Biography*, Anne Askew, 2016

Webb, Simon, *Life in Roman London*, 2017

Weinreb, Ben and Hibbert, Christopher, *The London Encyclopaedia*, 2008, 3rd Edition

Young, Elizabeth and Wayland, *London's Churches*, 1986

WEBSITES

www.cityoflondon.gov.uk
www.visitthecity.co.uk
www.cityoflondonguides.com
www.thecitycentre.london
www.stlawrencejewry.org.uk

Index

INDEX

INDEX

INDEX